Fatherhood

An Anthology of New Writing

Lee,

The bitter-sweet irony of fatherhood, and a few other factors like globe-trotting, is that you will finish this book before I do and I have owned my copy for over two years. It sits on the bedside locker and each evening I am to damn knockered to read anything.

Children are hard, really strength sapping time-sapping hard work but wow are they worth it ~~~~ smile when I get back from work ~~~~~~ d. Danny's feeble eff~~~~~~~tion are more joyous ~~~~~~~ Shakespeare. Aisling, e~~~~~~~~~~e in motion. You are a lucky ~~~~~~~~~~~e very, very best of luck, NICK.

D1166825

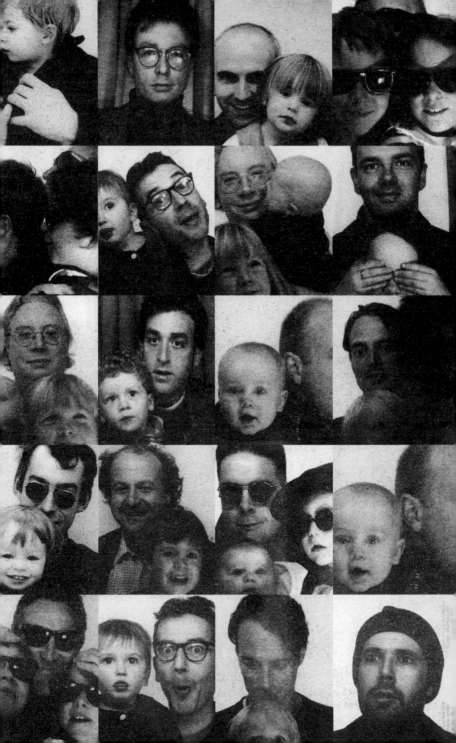

Fatherhood

An Anthology of New Writing

Edited by Peter Howarth

INDIGO

First published in Great Britain 1997 by Victor Gollancz

This Indigo edition published 1998
Indigo is an imprint of the Cassell Group
Wellington House, 125 Strand, London WC2R 0BB

The right of Peter Howarth and the contributors to be identified as
authors of this work has been asserted by them in accordance with
the Copyright, Designs and Patents Act, 1988.

A catalogue record for this book is available from the British Library

ISBN 0 575 40093 5

Lines from 'This Be The Verse' by Philip Larkin, first published in *High Windows*,
by kind permission of Faber & Faber Ltd.

Lines from 'A New England' by Billy Bragg are reproduced by kind permission of
BMG Music Publishing Ltd © 1983

Design and Typesetting by Digital Artworks Partnership Limited
Printed and bound by Guernsey Press Co. Ltd, Guernsey.

98 99   10 9 8 7 6 5 4 3 2 1

To Jackson, with love from your father

Contents

amazon.co.uk

GREETINGS FROM AMAZON.CO.UK

This item is not up to the quality standards Amazon.co.uk strives to meet. Because the supplier could not provide us with an item that met our standards, we have fulfilled your order with the best item available to us.

We know that in some cases getting an item in imperfect condition is better than not getting it at all, and our goal is to meet your needs.

If you are not satisfied with this item, we encourage you to take advantage of our returns policy, stated on the back of your packing slip.

Lee
— Dont worry about the quality, like everything else you own it will soon be covered in sweet-smelling baby sick.

Thank you for shopping with us!

Nick

Please send your comments to:
feedback@amazon.co.uk

amazon.co.uk
http://www.amazon.co.uk

Foreword

Peter Howarth

This book came about as the result of a conversation in a bar. Now before you reach for the sick bag, imagining a buddy-movie scene of men in their cups gripping each other's forearms and sincerely extolling the virtues of their offspring, let me reassure you: the conversation was between me, a man, and Liz Knights, a woman.

Liz, who has since sadly died, was at the time the editorial director of publishers Victor Gollancz and an old acquaintance of mine. We had met to catch up with each other's lives, and yes, I was talking about my recent entry into the state of fatherhood. She told me she had asked someone to write a book on the subject from the man's point of view, but he'd been unwilling. As we talked, we decided that what would be more interesting would be a collection of disparate essays on the topic – a dadly enterprise written for the amusement and, perhaps, edification of the recent father or father-to-be. She wondered if I might like to edit such a book.

Now – sick bags at the ready – I have to confess one of the reasons she may have thought I'd be up for the project, was that no doubt I'd been bending her ear about how my son's appearance in the world had changed my life irrevocably, extraordinarily and, to my mind, unquestionably for the better. I was then, and am still today, an unashamed dad evangelist. And I have had those conversations – the baby-bonding talk with other men – not just in bars and pubs, but also at work, in restaurants and in friends' kitchens and gardens. You see, in becoming a father I felt I'd been initiated into a secret society – a type of Masonic lodge where the only requirement for membership is the fact that you will never again be able to consider yourself a single, unattached member of the human race.

In fact, membership actually starts before the birth. I noticed something was up whenever I told another man I was about to have a child. Those without kids themselves would say things like, 'Oh, that's nice,' but clearly meant nothing by it. However, those already in the dad-lodge would smile a unique smile. No need to say anything: the look spoke volumes. It is a smile I have to say I've found on my own lips recently when confronted by some fresh-faced friend who proudly tells me of his good fortune. The smile says something like this: 'Welcome to the world of the father, where nothing is as it was. You may think you know now what it is to have responsibility, to be tired and wan, to be torn between the demands of the personal and the professional, to be unable to get anything organized because of the busy-ness of your hectic life. But let me assure you: as one who knows, I can safely promise you that at present you know *nothing at all.* And yet you are not only a man to be pitied, an innocent babe about to discover the true meaning of the word care. You are also to be envied – the luckiest man alive.' Imagine that in one smile – a combination of old-lag sympathy, empathy and patronage playing across the face of every father you meet – and you'll understand how daunting-intriguing the prospect of dadhood seemed to me.

By the time I was sitting with Liz in that London bar, I suppose my son Jackson was a few months old. The greyness that comes with sleepless nights was upon me, as was the addled philosophizing borne of the small hours of the morning, when I'd walk up and down the kitchen in an attempt to comfort my small boy. Liz was a canny woman and no doubt recognized the craziness and fervour in my eye which told her I was ripe for the task of corralling some old and new hands into writing for this anthology. And so I agreed to go in search of the voice of the modern father.

In the event it wasn't at all difficult. Every writer I spoke to who had children had something to say on the subject and, with few exceptions, none had ever been asked to commit their thoughts to paper before. I found this surprising but soon realized that parenting is a subject mostly written about by women for women from a woman's point of view. The role and experience of the father is occasionally addressed in a small chapter, but, by and large, motherhood is the subject of most child- and baby-care manuals. The dads I approached seemed only too pleased to be given the opportunity to sound off on the topic. This was an editor's dream; as was the fact that they all seemed to have diverse experiences to relate.

As the pieces started to come in, I realized too that unlike many subjects that men write on, fatherhood is not something they find it easy to lie about. By 'lie', I don't mean to imply that writers and authors habitually pass on falsehoods in their work, more that there is a male idiom that is full of bravado and swagger which is not entirely trustworthy. This is particularly the case with the new confessional-autobiographical style of writing you often find in today's men's magazines, Sunday newspapers and the odd book – where the authorial voice seems intent on persuading the reader that he is digesting the work of a good bloke who doesn't suffer too much in the face of the slings and arrows life chucks at him.

By contrast, the writing in this book strikes me as honest, often to the point of being painfully funny and revealing. Or just painful. Whether it be Tony Parsons explaining how his dad has influenced the way he treats his own son; Stephen Amidon on the disorienting experience of the delivery suite; or Carlo Gébler on the stepfather's tricky domain – the subject matter is clearly something that the writers of these pages found too important to trifle with. These are words from the heart as much as the head, and as such offer precious insights into the world of the modern father.

It only remains for me to thank all those who contributed for doing so in such good faith. And to thank Liz Knights for having given me the opportunity to explore an area I feel deserves a lot more consideration. I would also like to say a big thank you to my partner, Tracey Brett, for enabling me to become a father in the first place.

Robert Newman

Robert Newman's new novel, *Beat Surrender,* is out in the spring. He has written one other novel, *Dependence Day*, and is currently working on a film. For nine years he was a comedy writer and performer. He was forced to abandon his comedy career, sadly, upon receipt of an 800,000-signature petition. Robert Newman is compelled under Article 227b of the Geneva Convention on Human Rights 'to live by himself and not attempt — by way of advertisement, enticement or any other means — to share a flat with anybody else, male or female.'

And Now a Word From Our Spinster . . .

Robert Newman broods

'I was twenty-one years when I wrote this song,
I'm twenty-two now but I won't be for long.
People ask me, "When will you grow up to be a man?"
But all the girls I loved at school are already pushing prams.'

I used to find great consolation in those and other lonely-heart lyrics first heard in adolescence. Not any more. Not now that Billy Bragg is a father of two, and Barney Sumner has kids and Edwyn Collins has kids. Fuck me, even *Tom Robinson* is married with children! So what's my problem?

Women always say to me, 'You'd make a great dad,' but they never say, 'You'd make a great husband.' And that's the whole problem right there: here I am, single and childless, yet ineffably reassuring in a cardigan.

I want nothing more than to be married with children, but the trouble is that I'm being naturally deselected: my fear of commitment and the absent-minded trance I call consciousness have no place in the gene pool of a species with a tough future ahead of it.

When I die and grumpily slam the coffin-lid shut saying, 'Thanks for fuck-all, God!' He will be well within his rights to go, 'Whoah, whoah, whoah. Hold on. Didn't I send you Astrid O'Hurlihee, perhaps My Best Work Ever, who was, correct Me if I'm wrong, everything you ever wanted? And what did you do? Fuck-all is what.'

And He will be right. Fear and doziness and a gloomy fatalism made me feel I was being suckered into a *Play for Today* hell when really it was Act V of a romantic comedy, the happy ending, trumpets and strings. Fear paralyses the mind and I could only see the blessing that was mine when it was gone. *She* even thought I'd make a good husband ... but, seeing myself as a curse, if I really like someone I don't want to blight their life with mine.

The women are right with their dad/husband hiatus: I love almost all children but hardly any adults. I know what to say and do with children, but get it wrong all the time with adults.

And maybe I wouldn't be such a good parent, after all ... if I hate myself, how will I love a child who's a chip off the old block? (Plus I've always had a conviction that at least one of my children will be born horrifically deformed but that he will overcome his multiple disabilities to become a serial killer.)

I think broodiness in men is different from that in women. For me it's not about babies; it's when I see children five and upwards. Particularly neglected kids with matted, tatty hair and dirty faces. Kids whose parents don't take enough interest in them. Those are *my* children and I want to adopt them.

Broodiness is also a sense that without a wife and child I feel like I'm in the wrong place doing the wrong thing, like I missed my stop, like life has stalled, sputtering in an eerie silence. You may find yourself in a bachelor flat with filthy dishes on the floor and a clock ticking and you may say to yourself, 'Where is my beautiful wife? Where are my beautiful kids? This is not my flat. *Surely.*'

In my end is my beginning ...

I spent the first six weeks of my life in the Salvation Army Mothers' and Babies' Home in Hackney. My genetic father was an immigrant who'd been in England for four years. When he heard my teenage mum was up the stick he did not want to know. Unable to face me alone, after six weeks my mother, too, threw in the towelling.

If these haploid chromosomes of mine ever do go diploid, then that little baby girl (6–4) or baby boy (2–1) will be the first blood relation I've met since before my first birthday. I do hope I make a better job of it than the last time I met a blood relation. What a hash I made of it then! When I think about my behaviour during that crazy summer in the mid-sixties I hang my head in shame. Then, just like now, I failed to make a good impression on the woman I wanted to share my life with. I ruined my chances of happiness by an inability to see the nearest female as anything more than a brace of tits. What's more, I think I may have come across as being all 'Me, Me, Me,' Instead of thinking about *her* it was all 'I want! I want! I want!' All I ever thought about was, 'Where's my fucking dinner? I want my dinner NOW. And that means YESTERDAY, woman!' Add to that my bad hair and wobbly head movements and it's no wonder that she, like the ghost of girlfriends future, decided to try to find someone who was more the master of his emotions.

After a time, however, I had a National Insurance number and two people I could call Mum and Dad.

I loved Dad very much. He was hard-working, kind, warm, strong and sunny. A working-class man, he started off on the shop floor in television and radio factories. By the time I came on the scene he was boss of a hi-fi factory on the Holloway Road called Armstrong Audio.

He'd got to know about radios during the war. When he was seventeen he lied about his age, said he was eighteen and flew as a wireless operator in a bomber. The only time I ever remember him mentioning the war to me was when he told me that one of his jobs was to push parachutists out of the plane. I could have done with him in adult life, shoving me in the back when my nerve failed over the Dresden doll perfection of Astrid O'Hurlihee. Yes, I could do with him now, to let a little more air out of my inflatable armbands before pushing me into the shallow end of the gene pool.

I remember visiting him at the factory with my mum. There was a smell of soldering irons. Tall, beautiful women in saris made a huge fuss over me, treating me to hot lemon drinks from the vending machine.

He wasn't a political man and yet for some reason he was passionately anti-racist. A man at the factory told me about my dad shouting furiously at a man he had heard calling someone a wog or paki.

My uncle said, 'I didn't know he had lung cancer and when we moved house he was helping us carry heavy loads up six flights of stairs.'

I was nine years old and Dad's illness hit critical. I'd gone to sleep next door with Vic and Beryl. I forgot my pyjama bottoms and so had to sleep in my pyjama top and blue Y-fronts. When I went back next morning he was dead. At the funeral a huge crowd of beautiful women in saris were crying.

And so began a long and, of course, doomed search for a surrogate father, a role model, a masculine identity.

Being rather odd and not really belonging anywhere, my heroes have always been people who, unlike me, were very strong in their individuality. Steve Ovett, Muhammad Ali, Johnny Rotten. Men who knew who they were even if they had to change their names.

Not knowing who the fuck I am, I'm always looking for an answering voice: in music, in literature. And after Dad died I used to visit my Grandpop a lot.

Grandpop was my adoptive mum's stepdad. What me and Pop had in common was that neither of us was related to anyone else in the family. The other thing we had in common was that we both hated my new, tattooed stepfather.

Apart from the fact that he worked hard (as a shiftworker in a wall-paper factory where he was also shop steward), my stepfather was as unlike my dad as is imaginable: 'I tell you there's a touch of wog or diddicoy in that boy.' So I'd spend a lot of time at my Grandpop's at 118 the High Street. And it's only in writing this now that I realize how much of a surrogate father Pop was.

Grandpop was a cockney who'd worked his whole life at Smithfield meat market. He considered himself a Tory because the Duke of York had once shook his hand on a visit to the stalls. Grandpop wasn't a religious man, but he used to shout at the vicar in the street every time he saw him – religiously. When the vicar walked by Pop would open his front door and shout across the road, 'Call yerself a Christian! You do nothing for old people! I give them free tomatoes from my garden! Go on, go home to yer big 'ouse!' He had thick lenses in his glasses and with magnified, confiding eyes would lean towards me: 'Don't tell anyone – but I got this much in the bank,' he'd say, holding up four fingers. 'But I tell you who I wouldn't give my money to: Bradford & Bingley – they look like a right couple of idiots!' If Mr Bradford and Mr Bingley had walked past his house in their bowler hats he'd've opened the front door and told them so from across the road. He hated Alf Garnett but thought we ought to 'fly over Russia, drop a few bombs on them, show 'em who's boss'. His name was Ernie Bowyer. He taught me everything I know.

He had a chamberpot under the bed, a budgerigar perched on the frame of his glasses and white plastic rabbits in his back garden. He'd pour his tea into his saucer before drinking it to cool it down.

He didn't go to restaurants because, 'We went once and the food was so rich that as we drove away – and I've never done this before or since, have I, Sis? – I filled my pants. Now other people may care for that sort of night out but not us, so, no, we don't go to restaurants.' When my German exchange partner came with me to visit him, Pop recounted a First World War tale: 'I was walking past a cellar with my mate Borney and I said, "Do you think there's any Germans down there?" Borney chucks in a grenade and says, "Not now there ain't!" Ha ha ha! But we're all friends now, aren't we?'

When Nan – or Sis as she was known because she'd brought up her six younger siblings single-handed – fell over and couldn't walk, he wheeled her all the way to our house in a wheelbarrow.

For a time Nan and Pop took in an old cousin called Arthur as a lodger. A quiet man, Arthur used to sit at the kitchen table with his Woodbines, reading the *Daily Express* while Pop had his tea and filled in his pools. This arrangement carried on quite peacefully until one day Grandpop stood up and said, 'Get out! You never make any conversation! Get your stuff and get out!' I never saw Arthur again.

In his last years, when Grandpop got out of breath sweeping coal from the lino, he'd pretend to be humming a tune so I wouldn't hear how puffed he was.

The best touch was at the end. At Grandpop's funeral it was the same vicar who over the years had had to avoid using the High Street altogether – and he pretended they'd never met: 'I've heard from Ernie Bowyer's family that he was a very kind man ... apparently.'

I believe in Noam Chomsky's idea of genetically inherited patterns of language. It's only a small extension from that to a notion of a kind of genetic memory. I've got an idea that my blood grandfather was something like me. There's a comfort in that thought: I'm no longer a raving oddity, arms flailing in the wind, but part of a pattern, a continuation of something. Grandpa Chromosome was a Frenchman who moved to Cyprus where he sired my blood father – the running-away man (Nothing of me in *him*!) with his Greek-Cypriot concubine. Maybe Grandpa XY marks the spot where the writer in me comes from: an *émigré* not an immigrant. (But, then again, perhaps he was a sex criminal fleeing Interpol. I'll never know.) Often grandchildren more resemble grandparent than parent.

But you've got to be careful with grandparents. When I was in my twenties I tracked down Dad's dad who I hadn't seen since the funeral. 'Hello,' I said, when the broken recluse answered the door, 'I'm your grandson, Robert.'

'Well stone the crows, you better come in.'

We sat side by side in armchairs with a cup of tea and talked for hours. During this exchange I had a wondrous sense of belonging, of being connected to time past and time future. Eventually, however, during a lull in the conversation, my grandad turned to me and asked: 'Now let me get this straight – who are you exactly?'

It would be a very big thing for me to sire a blood relative, but that also makes it a fraught thing.

That said, I think perhaps my luck is about to change. I detect a change in the air ... All the single women my age have body clocks ticking so loudly that their questions are as abrupt and snappy as a bomb-disposal expert talking into his headset: 'Do you like children? ...How old are you? ... What's two and two?' Perhaps this will get me into the genetic play-offs – but I'm not convinced. Deep down I still feel that I'm being naturally deselected ...

The rest of you go on ahead. I'll hang back here. I'll find some soft limestone to bed down in and your descendants can dig me up in a thousand years and exhibit me: Non-Committal Man ...

'Note, students, if you will, the hang-dog expression, which years of erosion still haven't shifted; note he hadn't even washed up those broken earthenware pots; and note, finally, the skeletal fingers fixed in a death clasp round the TV remote and the other bony hand down the front of where his trousers once were.'

Charles Spencer

Charles Spencer is Theatre
Critic of the *Daily Telegraph*
and the author of two comedy
thrillers, *I Nearly Died* and
Full Personal Service, both
published by Victor Gollancz.
He married Nicola Katrak,
a principal dancer with the
Sadler's Wells Royal Ballet
in 1983. Nicki retired from
dancing in 1988. Their son
Edward, an IVF baby,
was born in April 1993.
They live in Claygate, Surrey.

Trying Times

Charles Spencer on when conception gets complicated

I suppose most of us, if we are lucky, are blessed with one golden summer, that moment when the Beach Boys' 'Good Vibrations' seems to sum up the meaning of life and anything seems possible.

Mine occurred in 1973 in a forlorn and neglected corner of south London which, in memory, still seems to shimmer and glow with heat. I was eighteen and had left school the previous December with a place waiting for me at Oxford that autumn. I'd just spent five months working, or rather skiving, in a tax office near my home in Surbiton.

The civil servants hadn't known quite what to do with a temporary intake of six students trying to finance their gap year, and had, very foolishly, put us all in a room of our own, leaving us to get on with the tedious business of form-filling, more or less unsupervised.

This we did, with great efficiency, for all of ninety minutes each day. The rest of the time was given over to cards, talk, an exhilarating sense of growing friendship and long liquid lunches in the nearby pub. We'd get down on our hands and knees after the pub had kicked us out and crawl beneath the window of the principal, who was nominally in charge of us, so he couldn't observe our lurching, giggly return after a three-hour session. It was bliss.

Of my five colleagues in that distant Eden, two are now dead. I've lost contact with the others, but one of them, Rosemary, still sometimes haunts my dreams.

Rosemary was beautiful, busty and, if truth be told, something of a stuck-up suburban prig. But the louche atmosphere of the great tax office skive seemed to rub off even on her, and I found myself falling in love with her. And then I pulled off my great coup which, even at this distance, still strikes me as being little short of miraculous.

My old school, Charterhouse, ran a mission in Bermondsey, south London, with a resident priest, community clubs and various other forms of worthy social work. I'd signed up to do two months' work in June and July, and in a moment of great daring I asked Rosemary if she'd like to join me. Amazingly, she agreed.

I'll spare you the details. Love's young dream can make for tedious reading. We were given a shabby flat in the mission house (with separate bedrooms) and we pottered around a vast local housing estate each day doing a survey on pensioners and asking them if they needed help of any kind. The idea of untrained teenagers from privileged backgrounds prying into the lives of poor but dignified south London oldies now seems unforgivably patronizing, but we were received with what felt like genuine warmth and the job was fun.

Even better fun was the fact that we two innocents wasted little time in relieving each other of our long-preserved virginity at last. We took clumsy 'precautions' with what were then known (to schoolboys, anyway) as 'rubber johnnies', and one night one of them burst. I don't think either of us was more than briefly anxious about this, but a couple of weeks later panic set in good and proper as Rosemary announced that she was late, most unusual for her, and might be pregnant.

The idea of confessing this to my parents (who'd never got round to telling me the facts of life), not to mention arranging an abortion, made me feel physically sick with anxiety. Rosemary retreated into a cold little world of her own and could hardly bring herself to speak to me. Our relationship, ecstatic on my part but always a good deal cooler on hers, I suspect, never really recovered from this trauma even when, a few days that felt like months later, she announced that all was well.

Yet even in the midst of that adolescent crisis, part of me, a small part admittedly, had been thrilled by the knowledge that I was capable of fathering a child. I never mentioned it to Rosemary, who brought up the idea of abortion very quickly indeed, but the thought of actually having the child didn't seem entirely preposterous either. It would mean giving up university, and a premature end to youth (though not to the tiny foetus I imagined in Rosemary's womb), but there would be something rather magnificent, even romantic, about becoming teenage parents. At that time, of course, I believed that Rosemary loved me almost as much as I loved her. Discovering that she didn't cast a shadow that made my earlier sun-lit happiness seem like the Lost Domain in *Le Grand Meaulnes.* Even the worry and the heartache were part of the wonder of that glorious summer.

If I've written at length about the events of more than twenty years ago, it's because for a long time I believed that the summer of '73 was as close as I was ever going to get to becoming a dad – even though it was no more than a commonplace teenage scare experienced by millions.

Unencumbered by a kid, I went to Oxford, and subsequently became a journalist, and it was while covering a tour of the Sadler's Wells Royal Ballet in the Far East that I met Nicki, the woman who was to become my wife.

Nicki was a rising star in those days, and for many years we didn't even discuss having children. She was made a principal ballerina in the year we got married, and though she often moaned about the demands of the dancer's life, she loved it too.

In 1988, however, she retired as a performer, and we decided, ghastly phrase, to 'start a family'. Nicki was in her early thirties, but we didn't anticipate any problem, though I occasionally wondered what the unnatural rigours of ballet might have done to her body. People were always asking if we were going to have children – an astonishingly personal question, when you stop to think about it, but one that is somehow deemed blandly acceptable, while asking people about their sex life, on which procreation depends, most certainly isn't. 'We're trying,' we'd reply, in the well-worn phrase and, over the next few years, it was all to become very trying indeed.

Each month, Nicki's period would start as regular as clockwork, and each month we'd try to kid ourselves that we'd never expected anything else. After eighteen months, however, we decided to see our GP, expecting to be told that such a long wait was nothing out of the ordinary. But far from offering comforting platitudes, our excellent doctor took one look at Nicki's age and decided we should see a specialist, since it was possible she might not have many years left for conceiving a child; if there was a problem it should be sorted out as soon as possible.

Our NHS specialist was a hatchet-faced East European who looked as though she might have enjoyed a more lucrative career playing sadistic villainesses in James Bond movies. She was about as comforting as a knock on the door from the Stasi in the middle of the night, and to hear her talk you'd think it was a miracle anyone ever managed to have children at all. Perhaps she was just trying to prepare us for the months and years of disappointment to come. I saw her a good deal less than my wife. Nicki almost invariably returned from her consultations in tears.

This Rosa Klebb of gynaecologists was very fond of producing diagrams of women's insides and explaining the mysteries of reproduction as if to a slow-witted child. She was even keener on temperature charts, which allegedly reveal the most propitious time for conception. Many fertility specialists now believe these are a waste of time and you should just have sex as often as possible if you want to have a baby, but for ages we timed our love-making to match the point where Nicki's temperature went up, which is supposed to signal the moment of ovulation. Rosa loved our charts, really loved them. Nicki drew them with the care of a swotty schoolgirl in the science lab, and they followed exactly the pattern they ought to. Unfortunately they didn't do the slightest bit of good, and having love-making determined by a thermometer wreaks havoc with your sex life. By now, having sex usually seemed like an unwelcome chore which invariably ended in disappointment.

Fairly early in the proceedings I was required to produce the first of many sperm samples for analysis. It goes without saying that the medical experts had wasted little time in stressing that sperm counts could be affected by smoking and drinking, and since I indulge in both, sometimes to excess, I feared the worst. I tried to cut down on both fags and alcohol for a few days before jerking off into my little plastic pot and rushing it round to the hospital lab for analysis. They need it within a couple of hours of ejaculation and you are supposed to keep the busy spermatozoa nice and warm. I tucked the little pot of spunk under my armpit for my walk to the hospital and felt like a prat.

A few days later I fumblingly opened the envelope containing the verdict on the test, feeling more nervous than when my A Level results flopped on to the doormat. At this stage I was fairly relaxed about not having a child, but Nicki was getting increasingly desperate. The idea that it might be all my fault, and a self-inflicted fault come to that, caused by too much self-indulgence, was ghastly to contemplate. And if they told me to cut out the booze and fags for as long as we were trying to have a child, would I be capable of exercising such self-restraint? I gloomily thought not, and saw a great vista of hellish guilt opening up before me.

In fact the sperm, bless them, were fine – healthy, mobile and in abundance. I felt indecently pleased about this knowledge that I was in full working order, but it put all the pressure back on to Nicki who was already suffering far more than I was.

In the early days, I had felt vaguely resentful that Nicki wanted a child so much. It would be lovely to have one, of course, but if we couldn't, surely we should just get on with things and make the best of what we had. We were happy, or had been until infertility entered our lives. Why should the absence of a baby matter so much? Wasn't I enough for her any more? I'd experience this nagging doubt a good deal, privately, and hated myself for such selfish and ignoble sentiments.

After an interminable wait – I dread to think how many women reach the menopause while being treated for infertility on the NHS – Nicki had a laparoscopy, a photographic probe which allows a clear view of the fallopian tubes and womb. While she was having this operation, Nicki was required to share a ward with a bunch of cheerful young mums who were surrounded by an unfeasibly large number of toddlers at visiting time. The tact of the NHS is boundless.

The news wasn't good. One tube was badly damaged, the other less so, but it wasn't certain that it was in a sufficiently good state of repair to let the eggs descend to the uterus. And it was at this stage, which we could have reached in weeks rather than a few years had we been treated privately, that IVF – or test-tube baby treatment as it is popularly known – entered our lives.

There was Christmas to get through first, though. By now, I wanted a child almost as much as Nicki, and when you are trying and failing to have children they seem to be everywhere. Crying on buses, beaming from advertisements, annoying their mothers in supermarkets and undergoing unimaginable suffering on the TV news bulletins. We'd almost stopped going to parties, because most of our friends had kids by now, and their homes always seemed to be knee-deep in mewling, puking little brats. What's more, my sister had just had a baby son. Damaged, jealous and inadequate as we now were, we couldn't face a family Christmas without a family of our own. Every time we saw a baby we felt like bursting into tears, a great ache of grief, like bereavement.

So we spent the festive season in Tenerife and ate our rubber turkey dinner with a couple with a fair claim to being the most boring people in the whole of Sweden. The merits of the Volvo can rarely have been more exhaustively debated. By now Nicki was taking fertility drugs for her first cycle of *in vitro* fertilization, and walking down the street or sitting in a bar, she'd suddenly inhale from a small bottle like a poppers freak. The holiday did us good, and we began to think of IVF with real optimism, even though we knew the chances of success were poor.

I had – and still have – real worries about IVF, a gut-feeling that it is somehow wrong to interfere with nature's course. If you don't have children, perhaps you are not *meant* to have children. How do you cope if, having officiously meddled with the natural order, the child you produce is physically or mentally handicapped? As I was writing this, there was a controversy about the fate of more than three thousand deep-frozen human embryos, created by IVF, now facing destruction because their parents hadn't come forward to express their wishes for their potential offspring's futures and the embryos' five year 'use-by' date was about to expire. They were indeed destroyed. What marvellous lives, deep frozen though they were, have been extinguished at the behest of bureaucrats.

Some of those caught up in that ethical dispute argued that the unclaimed eggs should be given to other infertile couples, and my first instinct was to say, of course they should – far better than to let them die. But without parental knowledge and consent on the part of those whose egg and sperm originally created the embryo, the baby who might eventually be born to another woman could grow up and meet his own twin sibling without any knowledge that they were related. If one were a boy, the other a girl, they might well feel instantly close to each other, fall in love and have children of their own, the offspring of unwitting incest. There is more than a touch of science fiction to the test-tube baby industry, and the implications are frightening.

Such scruples, however, begin to seem irrelevant when you watch the woman you love reduced, month by cruel month, to a state of clenched, unreachable anguish.

After two years of tests and gloomy prognosis from the NHS, the private IVF clinic was immediately welcoming. The staff were friendly, and the place seemed calm, well ordered and purposeful. Pictures of smiling, healthy IVF babies that had begun their lives there in laboratory dishes were displayed on the walls. One day, we thought, our son, our daughter, might be up there too. The IVF process itself also gave us the feeling that we were doing all we could to tackle the problem. It might not work, but at least we would know we had explored all the possibilities.

IVF is hellishly expensive, about £2000 a time, and several hundred quid more if a cost-conscious GP refuses to prescribe fertility drugs on the NHS as they sometimes, cruelly, do. A few months ago there was a news story about a woman who stole £20,000 from her employer but was spared a prison sentence when the judge, an unusually enlightened one, heard she had used the money to pay for test-tube baby treatment (it worked, I'm delighted to report). We could afford our treatments, just about, but I can't put my hand on my heart and say Nicki and I wouldn't have resorted to dishonesty if we'd been broke and had found an illegal opportunity of getting our hands on the cash.

The desperation of infertility is, I think, truly appreciated only by those who have been through the whole heartbreaking business. What's more, I feel like something of an impostor writing all this, because there is little doubt that women suffer far more than their men when they try and repeatedly fail to have a baby.

As someone who enjoys a gamble, I found the best way of handling the whole bizarre and ruinously expensive business was to imagine that IVF treatment was a form of roulette: a minimum stake of £2000 with the big pay-off of a child if your number came up. Even now, nineteen years after the birth of the first test-tube baby, Louise Brown, the odds are lousy. The average live-birth rate for IVF treatments in Britain in 1994–95 was 14.5 per cent. Some clinics managed almost 25 per cent; the worst managed less than 5 per cent. During our treatment we always thought our hospital had one of the highest rates of success, but I see from recently published data that last year it actually achieved only 9 per cent. IVF is big business and it was apparently not unknown in the past for clinics to massage their figures to attract punters to their high-stakes game.

For my wife, it was far harder to regard IVF dispassionately as a gamble against the odds. The fertility drugs, which I have a horrible suspicion come from human corpses, play merry havoc with the emotions as well as the hormones, and Nicki had to go to the doctor's each day for an injection like some helpless junkie. There were also regular, invasive ultrasound scans.

On the big day itself, however, when the woman's eggs are removed under anaesthetic, the onus is all on the chap. You have to produce your sperm on the hospital premises and the thought of humiliating failure in such desperate circumstances doesn't exactly set the libido racing. After producing endless samples over the years of treatment, I felt I could masturbate for England by now, but there were nevertheless some exceptionally dodgy moments.

On arrival at the hospital, while the woman gets enjoyably spaced-out on the pre-med, the man is dispatched to what I came to know as the wanking room. At our swanky hospital, it was got up to look like an anonymous four-star hotel room, complete with sofa, inoffensive modern art prints and expensive table lamps. I half expected to find a courtesy bowl of fruit and a mini-bar, and the latter would certainly have been most welcome. On one of the occasional tables a pile of well-thumbed soft-porn magazines is coyly placed. In one hand you clutch your little plastic pot, in the other ... well, you can guess the rest. Ridiculously, for a room entirely devoted to masturbation, there was no lock on the door. The memory of a nurse bursting in, without knocking, while I was in mid-wank, still brings me out in a hot flush of embarrassment.

Two days later, if the eggs have been satisfactorily fertilized by the sperm after being mixed together by white-coated technicians in the lab, the tiny four-cell embryos are placed in the womb. On the fourth treatment we saw them, three in number, projected on to a wall with a magnifying epidiascope. Our doctor thought one of them looked suspect, so only two were actually used: the thought that those two amoeba-like blobs might one day become babies was almost unbearably moving.

After the embryos have been put into the womb, the agonizing wait begins. Feverish hope alternates with a morbid conviction of failure, hour by hour, sometimes minute by minute. When it becomes clear that a treatment has failed – either because the woman's period starts, or following a pregnancy test at the hospital – the sense of desolation is indescribable. The emotional roller-coaster is so gruelling that both Nicki and I decided that we would make the fourth attempt our last – whatever the result. We simply couldn't take the pressure any more.

Nicki became increasingly convinced that it would be yet another failure. Oddly enough, seeing those strange, alien creatures on the wall of the hospital made her feel even more despairing. So near and yet so far. She decided that she wanted to be alone when the result came through to give her a chance to howl in peace, so I was packed off to France for a few days with a friend. I too was convinced of failure and got blind and maudlin drunk on the ferry and continued drinking deep into the night. The following day, horribly hungover, fearful and trembling, I phoned her from a Normandy seaside resort. She was officially pregnant, though the pregnancy would be precarious for the first three months. The hangover disappeared, just like that, and I tucked into a giant celebratory plate of *fruits de mer*.

In the early hours of 16 April 1993, Edward was born by caesarean section and I held him in my arms for the first time. What had once seemed like sinister science fiction now felt like nothing less than a miracle.

Edward is three now, and an absolute delight (well, most of the time, anyway). The other day we went to a funfair in Dorset and I took him on the dodgems. Afterwards he said that Sarsass would soon be along for his turn. 'Who's Sarsass?' we asked. 'My twin brother,' he replied, as if it were the most natural thing in the world. Nicki and I remembered those amoeba-like blobs on the hospital wall and caught a distant echo of a familiar pain. Grief, not for the dead, but for the unborn.

Douglas Kennedy

Douglas Kennedy is the author
of a novel, *The Dead Heart*,
and three travel books:
*Beyond the Pyramids, In God's
Country* and *Chasing Mammon*.
His latest novel, *The Big Picture*,
was published in May 1997.
The Dead Heart has recently
been filmed in Australia.
Born in New York City, in 1955,
he now lives in London with
his wife and two children.

Have I Got News for You

Douglas Kennedy learns he is to become a father

T ed Butt had terrific teeth – a cliff of white molars and incisors that were a testament to American orthodontics and steady flossing. Ted Butt had a very firm handshake and an air of easy bonhomie – the sort of fellow who'd greet you with a playful punch in the shoulder, then say 'Hey, fella!'

Tedd Butt was a team player – bright, but not particularly bookish; 'one of the guys' when it came to guzzling beer at a Saturday night barbecue, but sober and diligent come Monday morning. He was from the suburbs; he would end up back in the suburbs – a corporate man-in-the-making who, no doubt, would achieve partnership at some big law firm by the time he was thirty-three.

Indeed, from the moment I met him, I knew that Ted Butt would go far in American life.

We shared a suite of rooms during my final year at university. I had returned to the States after a stint in Ireland and – having forgotten to arrange housing for the academic year – found myself thrown in with Ted as a last-minute solution. We were unlikely room-mates. He was pre-law; I was pre-nothing. He hailed from some affluent bedroom community in Connecticut; I was a Manhattan boy who looked with disdain upon all things suburban. He went out with a string of blond, clean-limbed, deeply tanned women with names like Deb and Shannon; back then, I was chasing cerebral neurotics who always seemed to be gunning for the Sylvia Plath Emotional Stability Prize.

Despite our lack of common ground, Ted and I developed a curious rapport – and one which we both knew would never last beyond the year we'd spend sharing that suite of rooms. It certainly wasn't the sort of relationship in which we traded much in the way of secrets. We were nothing more than drinking mates – a couple of Buds, a couple of laughs. Until, that is, Ted ended his streak of cheerleader girlfriends and became infatuated with Barb Hoffman – an aerobically sleek Jewish American Princess with capped teeth, foghorn vowels and a way of talking that made the listener feel as if he were being assaulted by a verbal machine gun:

'So, like, I mean, I didn't ask my daddy to get me a BMW for my twenty-first, but it was, like, *there*, in black, my all-time favourite colour, and Mommy got me this cute little black Chanel bag to go with the black BMW ...'

I loathed her. And couldn't understand what Ted saw in her – besides the fact that she was a demi-babe. But there were plenty of other attractive women around college who didn't sound like a dentist's drill ... and who weren't walking proof of that old maxim: 'Capitalism is the process by which American girls become American women.'

Maybe it was the sex. The walls in our suite of rooms were notoriously thin – which made me an unwilling bystander to Ted and Barb's exceedingly loud coital activities. One night, while downing a jug of cheap Almaden wine with some budding performance artist (if I remember correctly, her name was Shelley and her 'act' involved eating dandelions to the sounds of a B-52 bombing raid), our conversation was suddenly silenced by a late-evening chorus of Ted's steady grunts and Barb's ever-increasing orgasmic moans. Eventually, this sexual soundtrack reached a crescendo – with Barb howling like a rabid wolf. Then there was silence. At which point Shelley turned to me and said:

'Sounds like she just dropped her magazine.'

On another occasion, while writing a term paper late into the night, the din of foreplay became exceedingly audible in the next room – sounds suddenly punctured by Barb's command:

'Do my breasts, Ted.'

Anyway, around two months into this exceedingly clamorous

romance, Ted staggered into the living room one night, looking as if he had just fallen into an empty lift shaft.

'You OK?' I asked, noting his shell-shocked demeanour.

'No,' he said, and asked for a whisky. I poured him an extra-large Jack Daniels. He took a very large gulp, then said:

'She just gave it to me.'

'Gave you what?'

'The news.'

'What news?'

'*The News.* She's pregnant.'

I refilled his whisky glass and poured one for myself. And after we had talked of matters like the unreliability of condoms, and the name of a good abortion clinic, Ted downed his bourbon, flashed me one of his team-player smiles, and said:

'Well, there's one good thing about this whole business. At least I now know that my guys can swim upstream.'

Fifteen years later, Ted's deeply inane comment suddenly sprang forth from some forgotten wastebin corner of my brain when I picked up my wife Grace from Gatwick. She'd been away on an extended three-week business trip to the Antipodes – and was looking uncharacteristically pale as she entered the arrivals hall. Driving back towards London, I mentioned the fact that she looked a little wan.

'Jet lag,' she said, then added, 'Oh, and I'm a fortnight late ... but I'm sure that it's just due to all the time zones I've been crossing.'

My hands tightened on the wheel. I gulped hard, trying to remain calm, all the while thinking:

'Jesus Christ. This is it. *The News.*'

There is, of course, something terribly appropriate about the discovery of impending fatherhood being referred to as *The News.* It sounds so ominous, so melodramatic, so terminal. You immediately envisage yourself in a doctor's surgery, watching with fear as your GP tears open a large manila envelope containing your most recent chest X-ray. Then he avoids your worried gaze and says:

'I'm afraid I have some news ...'

As your sphincter tightens, you suddenly find yourself wondering: how many months do I have, exactly?

Of course, as an impending father, you know the answer to that question. It's nine. Or, if you prefer, 40 weeks. Or 280 days. Which, in turn, is 6720 hours. Or 403,200 minutes.

Indeed, you become very conscious of time when you hear The News. Because you feel as if you are living under a sort of death sentence. I know that sounds a little theatrical – but I certainly felt as if some Islamic cleric had just put a fatwa over my head. I was a condemned man. My independence – my ability to jump on a plane at will and vanish into some back-of-beyond corner of Egypt – was at an end. I had entered the last nine months of personal freedom. After that child arrived, I was certain that I would be confined to a gulag of nappies and night feeds and terminal sleeplessness and general domestic chaos.

'The test turned pink, and you turned grey,' Grace later noted. Indeed, my eyes did glow wide as the Boots' dip-stick transformed itself into a nice pastel Laura Ashley colour (suitable, no doubt, for a nursery). At the same time, however, I did hear a distant echo of Ted's voice in my head:

Well, at least my guys can swim upstream.

Ah yes – here it was. Irrefutable proof that all those dental X-rays I'd received as a kid hadn't wreaked havoc with my sperm count. But rather than feeling some sort of macho triumph ('I'm firing on all cylinders!'), all I could think was:

A father? Me?

I didn't fit the bill. As a child I'd grown up in a decidedly stormy household – and besides discovering the pleasures of my own company, I had also developed a strong resistance to family life. Children, to me, were a synonym for discord. They caused unnecessary friction. They drained your financial and emotional resources. They confined you to one spot.

In shops or restaurants, on planes and trains, the ongoing sobs of a child had always made me grind my teeth and wonder how anyone could put up with the little bastards. They turned their parents into indentured servants. They were temper-tantrum terrorists who wailed until their demands were met.

Now, of course, I felt something akin to despair as I watched a haggard father trying to negotiate with his tired and emotional three-year-old who'd just decided to throw a tantrum in front of the chicken tikka masala at Marks and Spencer. '*That's gonna be you, pal,*' said a taunting little voice inside my head. And I began to wonder if the *Légion étrangère* would allow an unfit 37-year-old to join their ranks.

Of course, all those thoughts of flight – of telling Grace I was going to the corner shop for a Hamlet cigar and then running for the next plane to Mauritania – were mere melodramatics. Men, after all, are deep emotional cowards. And while we all spout on about the need for liberty, the lure of the road, the desire to sleep with every hooker in a Shanghai cat house, we spend much of our lives digging ourselves deeper and deeper into a familial cul-de-sac of our own making. I once had a professional acquaintance who always moaned on about how he hated his staff job on a national newspaper, how his wife was now about as sexually appealing as a roll of cling-film, and how, ever since the birth of his first son, he was fiscally strapped beyond hope.

'Every time I go to the cash machine, I have this desperate moment when I wonder: will it grant me a few quid to stagger through the day?'

Yeah, he was something of a self-pity specialist – especially since his solution to his alleged domestic nightmare was to have two more kids within the space of three years. He hated his confinement, yet he also needed it. Craved it, in fact. That's the thing about most men – they like the idea of flirting with jeopardy, of putting everything at risk ... but, simultaneously, they fear the loss of emotional ballast. To use a bad building metaphor for a moment, they often feel like kicking down a wall, but then also dread the idea of the entire edifice they've built tumbling down atop their heads.

Have you noticed, for example, how men always dither when they're ending a relationship – how, having hinted that they want out, they then keep hovering around the scene of their most recent romantic disaster, like a dog returning to sniff its own vomit? Women, on the other hand, usually have a far more stoical attitude towards matters of the heart. They will put up with countless stupidities and petty betrayals for years. But then, when they finally resolve to give you the heave-ho, the shutters come down and the 'Out of Business' sign is posted by the door. And no matter how hard you try to plead or cajole, you know that you're not going to be allowed on the premises again. Their decision, once made, is final.

Men, however, revel in emotional indecision. Especially when it comes to receiving The News. My father, for example, admitted that, after hearing my mother was pregnant, he thought, Why didn't I become a homesteader in Alaska?

His comment made me laugh. Because, after watching that Boots' dip-stick go pink, I also started thinking things like, Maybe it's about time I gave up book writing and started covering wars.

But I never sought out a journalistic stint in Sarajevo – just as my father never ended up in glacial moose country north of Fairbanks. Because we both secretly knew that there was a troubling underside to the business of running away – the haunting thought of what life would have been like had you stayed.

That's the thing about The News. You fear it, but you're also curious to discover how you will cope with this new-found state of fatherhood. As any third-rate anthropologist will tell you, reproduction is the primary function of our time on earth (to which the reaction of most childless guys must be, 'OK ... but the future of the planet doesn't come down to *me*'). Surely, so the logic goes, you must want to see what you've spawned ...

Of course, you also know that the relationship with your squeeze (or 'partner', for the politically correct among you) is about to enter new, uncharted territory. And even if, like me, you made certain that you didn't marry a carbon-copy edition of your mother, you secretly fear: will she suddenly turn into some sort of maternal obsessive? Will the arrival of a third party in our midst cause irreconcilable tensions? Will we – amidst the chaos of parenthood – lose sight of each other?

Indeed, with The News comes the belief that you can forget all notions of fun for the next twenty years – by which time your children will be making reverse charge calls from Goa, demanding that you wire them a thousand quid, while also telling you how you ruined their lives. And you come to hate all those blissful Celebrity Parents you see profiled in the pages of glossy magazines, pontificating on about the 'fulfilling centrality' of children. Of course, children are fulfilling – especially if you have a platoon of Latin American nannies to get up with them at night.

The News, in short, is a code-word for fear. All your insecurities – about your ability to earn a living, to sustain a long-term relationship, to have even one-tenth of the maturity and competence necessary to raise a child – come to the fore.

And then the child arrives and you make an intriguing discovery: this thing called parenthood isn't such a daunting business after all. You can handle its pressures. Your marriage doesn't come asunder. You realize that it is curiously gratifying. Yet, secretly, you find yourself still dreaming of the empty highway, the tropical atoll, the one-way ticket to Patagonia. Because, for most of us, good news is always hard to accept ... or even recognize.

Nicholas Lezard

Nicholas Lezard was born in
1963 and his daughter was
born in 1995.

Baby on Board

Nicholas Lezard defines
the gulf between the
haves and the have-nots.

'I wish either my father or my mother, or indeed
both of them, as they were in duty both equally
bound to it, had minded what they were about
when they begot me; had they duly considered
how much depended upon what they were then
doing; – that not only the production of a rational
Being was concerned in it, but that possibly the
happy formation and temperature of his body, perhaps his genius and the very cast of his mind ...'

Laurence Sterne, *The Life and Opinions of
Tristram Shandy*. Vol. 1. Chap. 1.

Humanity has plenty of fault lines, God knows, but one of the
deepest ones is that between parent and non-parent. It is a divide so
large that we deny, most of the time, that it is there, which is odd,
because we spend all our time being parents or not being parents,
much as we spend all our time being gay or straight, or black or
white, or male or female. It brings to mind the psychoanalytical

shorthand term for denial: the elephant in the bedroom, or something so present, so enormous, that the best way of dealing with it is pretending it isn't there (not, when one considers it, the worst way of dealing with a big problem).

This divide – parent v non-parent – can be an unsettling thing to admit, because it says something worrying about what should be a matter of common consent, or unified will (one may as well say that there is a split between people who like air or sunlight, and those who don't): so approach the business sideways rather than head-on. Look, or remember looking, at a photograph of your parents taken before you were born. It can be disconcerting, this reminder that they had lived before you, and it's not just that they look younger, less careworn. They look palpably different. The world around them is bizarre, historical. And the *idea* of them is also bizarre: you feel like chivvying them, grabbing them by the shoulders and telling them, like Tristram Shandy, to *think*.

'Before you were a twinkle in your mother's eyes', or more bluntly, 'while you were still swimming around in your father's balls', are usually delivered as rebukes to someone deficient in experience and perspective; and, like so many rebukes, they can be exasperatingly counter-productive. We end up doing important things without thinking (it really is exquisite, the life-long trouble that a brief and irresponsible act of carnal indulgence can let us in for). Children seem to know this, and as a result are natural solipsists: one three-year-old of my acquaintance extends her solipsism to the created world, and is given to explosive outbursts of rage when anyone alludes to anything that happened before she was born.

She's right to do so, because she recognizes that there is a deep rift between the world that predates her and the world that includes her: the former is a con-trick, she argues, like creationists who claim that dinosaur fossils were stuck into the earth by a prankster God, like so many sixpences in an enormous Christmas pudding. I can imagine that my parents had a life before I was born; but then I can also imagine the universe's fourth dimension – which probably means that I am not imagining it correctly. And so, in the last days of non-fatherhood, I would look at everything about me, all the objects I had acquired over the years, the fragments I had shored up against my ruin, and imagine little hands ruining them, tearing everything down, the record collection, the photo albums, not just because they were there but because they were there *before*: when I was not a father, and had no reason to exist. Like Pol Pot, children start at Year Zero.

Thoughts like these made me feel very uneasy about becoming a parent. I recognized that something was going to happen to me which would change my identity in a way that had not happened before; the lurch from childhood to adolescence seems leisurely, protracted in comparison, not only because it takes more than nine months, but because, after all, it is the same mind that experiences the change. Parenthood involves the intimate involvement of another life. One stops doing everything for oneself and starts doing it for someone else.

Being a selfish and lazy person, this idea gave me, to put it mildly, the willies. What would have to happen to me, at a cellular level, to change me from a dissolute young hedonist to a responsible parent? I recall the sense of impatient disgust that I felt, child-free, when visiting friends with an infant. All those bright plastic toys scattered round the room; mobiles, crayon scrawls taped proudly to the fridge; the bath cluttered not with the genteel impedimenta of singlehood (a tasteful shaving set, the odd bottle of hair tonic, a little wicker basket of pot-pourri), but with a boat-load of daft toys, stylized whales, the rubber duck not ironically placed, but horribly pertinent, and yelled for if missed; the impossibility of maintaining a conversation for more than three minutes without being interrupted by the demands of a child; the impossibility of maintaining an adult conversation, full stop. Nappies – dear God, *nappies* ... How could the parents bear to live like this?

And worse, the way they talked about the love they felt for their child, that unassailable devotion, the uncritical vocabulary that goes with it ('the mother's brains exit along with the placenta', ran one joke I heard) ... it made me puke and, judging by the streaks of baby-vomit running down the shoulders of every parent's shirt, it seemed to be making the children puke too. A father told me of how he had scooped out a fist-sized turd from his baby's anus with his fingers, mindful of how one false or unlucky move could cause the rectum to prolapse; another advised using a parsley stalk in the same place, as one would a pipe cleaner. I had heard enough. *Basta*.

Then my wife got pregnant. It must be said that it was not entirely her fault. I had a hand in it, so to speak; but while a shadow might have flitted across my mind at the relevant moment, it wasn't anything that would have satisfied young Shandy, born into a scurvy and disastrous world some nine months later. The old saying has it that a stiff prick has no conscience; this could be amended to 'a stiff prick has no knowledge or sense of the future'; which is maybe all that conscience is.

The surest, most unshakeable analogy I could make (and still can make) about the difference between the way one is when not a parent and the way one is when one is, is the difference between the people in *Invasion of the Body Snatchers* before they get taken over by the alien pods, and the way they are after. They struggle like wolves to keep themselves the way they always have been; and, after it happens, they insist that they are now perfectly happy, a lot happier than they were before, in fact, and it would be a good thing if you just settled back and tried not to fight it. (The same kind of philosophical question about our identities happens in the kind of films where the evil doctor is about to administer a syringe full of mind-altering stuff to our hero, strapped and sweating in a dentist's chair. You know the kind of thing I mean.)

So now I speak as a parent. I coped with the nine months of grace by writing a humorous diary of the gestation, from my point of view, for a magazine; but behind the humour was the intent to show a person (me) in flux: changing from one thing to another. From someone like Dr Johnson, who once threw a woman and her baby out into the snow from the stagecoach they were travelling in because she started going coochy-coo at her child; to someone who'd start going coochy-coo himself. (And think of that term 'coochy-coo': used with contempt by young males to describe the ludicrous attention paid to manifestly inferior beings.)

Writing that diary (working title: 'How To Be a Pregnant Man') was itself a bit of a cheat. I stopped it, quite deliberately, at the point where I was scraping the ice off the windscreen prior to the final drive to the hospital. Anything that happened behind the doors of the delivery room, and certainly anything that happened after the child was clear of the labia, was no one else's business, but I also felt that it was important to write prior to the deep, fundamental change that was happening to me. And although technically during the writing of the diary I was a non-parent, the polishing-up and the conclusion were done by someone else: a parent. So I was already breaking my own rules. Which in itself felt like a useful lesson in parenthood: how to dissemble for the sake of the child; how to fudge the issue of issue.

Of course, there is no real fundamental change at all. At least not in the father. There is change, plenty of it – but it is all at the superficial level. This might seem odd, and definitely counter-intuitive in my case, where literally overnight I changed from the kind of man who scoffed at 'Baby on Board' stickers to – on driving back from the hospital with the new baby in the front seat – the kind of man who wanted 'Baby on Board' displayed on both the back window *and* the windscreen. But the man's character only changes in the manner of the rat who has been taught to run through a different section of the maze. The chemical soup sloshing around in him is still the same, a feeling one cannot hold with the same certainty about the mother, who, for the most part, takes the paradigm shift in reality with contemptuous ease, for all that she claims to be as unprepared as you are, as shocked and disappointed that a little manual doesn't plop out on the delivery bed after the baby. The baby's arrival has answered a need, probably hormonally inspired, that has been nagging at the mother-to-be for – well, it could have been for years. For all that I know, the cells of a woman who has given birth are different, under the microscope, from those of one who has not; the man's are resolutely the same for ever.

(And yet I have not, with an instinctive capacity for restraint that continues to astonish me, ever uttered the line, when faced with an awkward request for my babysitting time, or other rearing-related effort asked of me at an awkward moment, 'No, *you* do it – you're the one who wanted the child, after all.' No book has taught me this, nor have I heard it from anyone else – but then I don't know how I could have worked it out for myself – it must be one of those minuscule data of fatherly knowledge that are actually inherent, genetic. I just know it to be fundamentally true. I'll repeat it, in clearer syntax: never, ever, however much you want to, ever say words which mean anything like the following to the mother of your child: 'No, *you* do it – you're the one who wanted the child, after all.' Got that? Say 'I'd love to, but I'm frightfully busy' instead, if you must; but save yourself a lot of bother and say 'yes'.)

What I think I am leading up to is that the experience of fatherhood is more instructive than that of motherhood. Motherhood is a given, an automatic duty. The mother who leaves her baby in a cardboard box drives us into a frenzy of speculation and despair; a father who did the same wouldn't even make the local news. You may speculate on the male's native fecklessness by reflecting that, at the precise moment of writing these words, i.e. generalizing about fatherhood with a specious air of authority and experience, I am safely locked up in my studio, while downstairs my wife and three other women are actually getting on with the business of keeping their children entertained, not to say alive. It is not even a particularly rich irony, that is the pity of it.

But I am not alone; and I can't help feeling that, in a funny way, we are all fathers now, mystified or even outraged by the demands that being a parent place on our precious lifestyles. Feeling society's pulse, you can get a sense that we are becoming less family-orientated; which is another way of saying that we are having fewer children. We don't want them around so much; they cut into our time. (Remember that, as far as the middle classes go, we are only a couple of generations in to being woefully underserved by the army of nannies and general staff that kept our ancestors from doing their nuts when trying to juggle jobs and teach little Timmy to mind his Ps and Qs; no wonder, except for the indecently wealthy, we haven't quite got the hang of it yet.) The latest technological advances which everyone yaks on about – specifically the Internet, CD-ROMs and 500-channel TV – are 'cultural' developments whose pulling power is predicated on their ability to keep our attention engaged *for every single minute of the day*; and in fact there is a sense that if one does not spend an enormous amount of time with them, one is under-utilizing their potential (you might as well be a technosaurus, with a manual typewriter and a dial telephone). It is no accident that the appeal of the new frontier lies primarily with adolescents, or people with adolescent frames of mind: for the adolescent, like a character from Beckett, is always mindful of being at the edge of a huge abyss of tedium, which only a superabundance of information, pornography and music videos will keep him (yes, it's usually *him*) from falling into. Nor is it an accident that the emperors of the new millennium are popularly perceived as being social autists.

These twenty-first-century paradigms could not have been devised by a conscientious man helping to bring up children. The ideal, clean world of satellite feeds and chirruping modems does not sit easily with the world of bodily effluence, and patience and responsibility in the face of total ignorance that you are thrust into when up against your own offspring. You are, all of a sudden, in the real world. The CD player in your Ford Probe might have crystal-clear sound and vibrant, pounding bass, delivering sound quality our ancestors never dreamed of, but for the parent, *Homo Sapiens Sapiens* is still brushing the flies from his face at the waterhole (and you can knock off that second 'sapiens' while you're about it; maybe even the first). The childless could be forgiven for thinking that procreation is an activity confined to some new kind of underclass. Have you ever wondered why it is that while human ingenuity has made this century the finest time, so far, to be alive on earth – when everything has been made easier: travelling, getting food in your mouth, having a bath, a tonsillectomy, you name it (assuming you do not come from the Third World) – that rearing children seems to have become more difficult, more fraught with anguish? The only exception to this is the disposable nappy – and it is a testament to our irresponsibility and craving for convenience that we are happy to cover the earth with used Pampers for the sake of a little extra time, and a little less cack, on our hands.

We can peer at viruses through electron microscopes but we still despair when it comes to turning little Timmy into a functioning member of humanity. And our despair is getting more acute as we become aware of the growing number of people who are *not* turning into functioning members of humanity. It seems logical to blame bad parenting for this, and bad fathering in particular (although we may be wrong about the proposition, never mind its imagined cause). Why do you think you are reading this book? You are looking for some clues, some reassurance, maybe even some light relief from the ordeal ahead; but it wouldn't be in your hands right now if you thought you had all the answers. (All areas of ignorance and fear are breeding-grounds for charlatans: this is why a new theory of child-care is born every four minutes.)

Neither would you be reading this book, or this sentence, if you were childless and intending to remain so. The areas of experience that delineate the parent from the free are not just internal, they're geographical: the children's and parenting sections of bookshops (surprisingly large, you discover), those shelves in supermarket and chemist given over to formula milk, wipes and nappies. There's no doubt about it: you lot without children – you don't know you're alive. I mean it. Child-free, you can absent yourselves from the world all day long if you really want to. With a child – forget it. You're in it up to your elbows. Even the most slothful and lackadaisical father – that's me, although there are worse specimens, but then they are only fathers *de jure*, and I look down on them the way the old lag in the Scrubs looks down on the nonce – will get some shit under his fingernails at some point. And until Huxley's new world of factory-farmed babies comes to pass, things will stay that way. I mention shit, by the way, to drive home how elemental this business is. I found myself, while the shock of scraping the stuff out of my child's vagina was still fresh in mind, suddenly ashamed and disgusted the next few times I went for a crap myself. This was a new one on me. Me and my shit had until that point got on fine.

We'd grown up together. We knew each other's place. But now shit had entered my world – new shit – and I can't say I liked it. You too may find, as I did, during that phase of children's development when their shit comes out as a greenish paste, that you cannot bring yourself to eat pesto. Eventually this phase goes and you find instead you cannot eat anything brown and chunky for a while, like a nice *boeuf en daube.*

This might all strike you as being a bit negative, that I am not exactly enjoying all this. Permit me to correct you, and to say that I am well pleased in my child, that I am a fool for her love. This love is perhaps the strongest cause of the distrust and suspicion that exists between our two rival humanities: for no one loves this much, this continually, until one has a child. It is understandable for someone to feel miffed when they are, by implication, accused of being deficient in this respect, and that is why this love has become, like homosexuality used to be, the love that dare not speak its name. Like many such loves, of course, when it does speak its name you wish it would shut up; but I am going to have to give you a brief run-through here. (The squeamish may avert their eyes.) I have begun to understand the deep devotional bond between parent and child; I begin to understand the reality behind the phrase that comes off the lips of so many besotted parents: 'I could eat you all up'. For the love is like some ravenous hunger that can never be satisfied; when Kronos devoured his own children I imagine that the reasons given – that he did not want to pass on his inheritance (the universe) to them – was something of a blind. And just as there is something elemental, preconscious and involuntary about this love, so it feels, at times, as if you have been given a kind of superhuman power, a strength, an intimation of immortality, at the same time as you have become weakened, frightened and all too conscious, as you look at the future represented by your own child, that you really *will* die (yes, it's finally beginning to hit home). You might, on entertaining an unruly infant in Pizza Express, be subjected to the baleful stares of the child-free: they are nothing compared to the baleful stares you can give back. My child bothering you? Pal, you are mistaking me for someone who gives a shit.

Yes: it *is* different. The difference is so extreme that the only metaphors which do it justice are those from science fiction or fantasy: the journey through the stargate in *2001*, the shift from black-and-white to Technicolor in *Oz*, the transformations of the Body Snatchers. The difference is in the fabric of reality; our character, our *contemporary* character, is tested, and not always within endurance, by the arrival of a child, the way it would be changed if we lost our legs, or our sight; and I don't make that comparison facetiously. What you lose, definitely, assuming you have any sense of decency or responsibility at all, and you can't afford the help, is your capacity for mobility. Yet, like the handicapped, we have our own sense of dignity, of self-worth. Alien to the rest of you, I know; but still there.

I take a look at my previous self's gravestone: Non-father, 1963–95. Occasionally, and with gradually decreasing frequency, I toss a few flowers on it or have a little sniffle. There were a few things that guy wanted to do, but he left them too late ... now he'll never get the chance. But on the whole I don't mind. I'm thinking of my little daughter, who, at our suggestion, goes 'beep beep' when she presses the tips of our noses, as if she's ringing a buzzer. Just the other night, we'd put her to bed, and there she was in her cot, pressing the tips of her toys' noses and going 'beep beep'. Do you find that too nauseatingly cute? Do you not want to live in a world where you find such moments touching and meaningful, a world in which the preservation of innocence becomes, all of a sudden, a priority? Where the place you live in stops being wholly playground for adults and starts becoming something like the child's world, playground too but also infused with danger and menace? Where you stop darting across the road but instead, when pushing a buggy, go fifty yards out of your way to find a pelican crossing? Where you notice that Alsatians' teeth and car exhausts are at the same height off the ground as a buggy-bound child's face? Perhaps you find my eyes a little strange, a little too glittery and dead at the same time, my beatific expression too fixed, unreal. You find the grip of my hand on your shoulder disconcertingly powerful, and notice, suddenly, other shadowy men around you with the same expression, carrying sinister little bundles. My arguments strike you as rambling, incoherent, strange tendrils of thought failing to connect with each other. Fear not: this is only lack of sleep. Join us, I say, join us: you won't regret it. You'll like it once it happens to you, you'll *like it*, honest you will ...

And meanwhile, like the last man in *Invasion of the Body Snatchers*, someone out there is running through the traffic, crying, 'Watch the skies ...' Only it isn't spaceships he's telling you to watch out for: it's storks, flapping with their heavy burdens to your very homes.

David Thomas

David Thomas was born in 1959. An award-winning journalist and former editor of *Punch*, he has written extensively about men's issues, most notably and controversially in his 1993 book, *Not Guilty: The Case in Defence of Men*. His satirical novel *Girl*, about a young man caught in a hospital mix-up, who is accidentally given a sex-change, was translated into six languages and is currently being adapted as a film. He lives in Sussex with his wife Clare, and their two daughters, Holly (right) and Lucy (left).

The Name Game

David Thomas on the problems
of choosing a moniker

My house is full of names. I'm David – and never, ever Dave,
if you know what's good for you. My wife is Clare – note: no 'i' in
the middle. We've got two dogs: a sad-eyed cocker spaniel called
Mozzy (short for Morrissey, the singer, who was also, for reasons too
complicated to go into now, a sort of family pet) and a bouncy black
Labrador called Rowdy.

There are four cats: Bollinger, Guinless (so-called because he's
black and white, daft and has had his guins chopped off), Freebie
and a little tabby kitten called Gus, who's also known as Scrappy-
Doo. There are four guinea-pigs: Habit, Dolly, Buzz and Jiff. Sadly, we
had to sell Sniffy and Niblets.

The chickens, all twelve of them, don't have names, because
I can't bear to eat any animal I've known personally. But in the
days before such squeamishness prevailed, we had three beautiful,
golden-feathered buff Orpingtons called Christie, Nadja and Claudia,
a red-headed pullet called Linda and another all-black bird called
Naomi. These, of course, were the Supermodel chickens, and let me
tell you, boys, they were brilliant layers.

We've got two children too – girls aged seven and eight – and this
is where it all becomes tricky. Anyone can name a pet. You can give

them any old handle, no matter how ridiculous, and they'll never complain. If it turns out you've made a mistake, or you get bored, just change the damn thing. Trust me, animals don't know the difference.

But kids are different. Children's names are the cause of agonized hours of self-interrogation, heated debates, intractable family rows. Give your offspring names they hate, and they'll resent you for ever. They, after all, are the ones who have to walk into the playground and say, 'Hi, I'm Tarquin'. Or Boudicca. Or any of the other stupid names that pretentious middle-class parents dump on their nippers because they're too bloody chi-chi just to call the poor little blighters Bob or Jane.

My grandmother wanted me to be called Godolphin. She came from a smart West Country family. Her folks had been Lord-Lieutenants of Devon for more than five hundred years. They'd lived on the same estate outside Exeter since 1067. My grandfather, however, was a bank clerk from Cardiff. At school, he had been known as Thomas 17. He was David, too, like his father and his son. All the first sons of the family were David. But when I was born, my grandma was determined to end the tradition.

In part, her reasons were practical. It was a nuisance trying to run a household in which all the menfolk had the same name. Anyone familiar with Dr Seuss's poem about Mrs McCave, who had twenty-three sons and she named them all Dave, will know what I mean (except that none of us were Dave, of course). And besides, David Thomas was a common little name, and she wanted a reminder that she, at least, came from purer stock than we lowly Welshmen.

Because in this country, names – like practically everything else – denote class. And age. And race. Even if you're Caucasian, they describe the part of Britain from which you come. If I say, 'Herbert Ramsbottom', you think, Daft old bugger from the North. If I say, 'Meet my children, Thurman and LaRochelle', I may very well be black. Interestingly, though we know that names like Sandip or Asish are Asian, the chances are we don't know any more than that: white society hasn't yet tuned into the nuances of Asian culture. We can't yet tell the Sikh from the Muslim, or the Brahmin from the beggar.

But we can sort the Sloane from the Essex Girl all right. My first serious girlfriend was the stepdaughter of a housemaster at school. She was called Iona Stormonth-Darling. I have seen shop assistants start sniggering at the very sight of her name on a cheque. You can't blame them I suppose – it just screamed out, 'I am a toff'. Years after we'd broken up, Iona got married ... to a bloke called Cobb. Now she's nicely anonymous.

Contrariwise, anyone called Darren, Wayne, Sharon or Tracey might as well go right ahead and have the word 'common' tattooed on their forehead. Because, the instant prejudices of the British being what they are, that's what everyone's thinking. Mind you, those are all names that are time-specific, too. Primary school class-rooms these days are filled with pop-culture names like Kylie (watch out for a million Liam and Noels coming up soon), or nob names moving downmarket, like Charlotte, or Sophie. In forty years' time, Wayne will seem as genteel and elderly as Winifred does now.

Even those of us whose names are nondescript give away clues by other means. David Thomas is bland enough. But wait. My initials are D. W. P. I have three Christian names – a dead giveaway of an upper-middle-class background.

My second name is William. My third name is Penrose. Just imag-ine the shame of that. Imagine the years I spent praying that my classmates would never find out, the amount of forms I filled in as 'David William Peter'. Because Penrose, as any schoolboy knows, is a poof's name. And poofs are cissy, and almost as bad as girls. So you should beat them up, just to be on the safe side.

Christ, I'm glad I've never had to name a son. For just as we men are limited in the clothes we can wear, the things we can do, the way we can talk, or any of the other restraints that are imposed upon us in order to keep us within the safe, sterile boundaries of convention-al masculinity, so we dare not fool around with names.

If we had had a boy, I was all for copping out and calling him David, just like everyone else. Clare, though, wanted to ring the changes. But to what? Inspired by Bryan Ferry's choice of name, we toyed with the idea of naming our nipper Otis. We reckoned Otis Thomas sounded pretty cool. Which it would have done, had our little Otis been the son of a super-chic, lounge-lizard rock-god. Or a running-back for the Dallas Cowboys. But the odds were he'd spend his childhood as a speccy, spotty, scrawny little swot, just like his dad. And though that's undoubtedly a Thomas, it sure as hell ain't no Otis.

So we decided to go for something really basic. Like James, or Freddie. I love the way that French films always seem to have heroes called Fred, or Bob, which they pronounce 'Bubb' in a cool Gallic way, just like the girls in Bond films always call him 'Chems'. But then again, the most popular name in France right now is 'Kevin', so what the hell do they know?

The question I always asked myself was, 'Does he seem like a nice bloke?' Freddie Thomas, for example, would be the life and soul of the party at a public school – although my kids are educated courtesy of the State, and he'd have had a harder time there, I fancy. Plus, Freddie doesn't sound particularly serious when it's time for that crucial job interview; Frederick's a bit poncey, and as for plain Fred, well, Fred West, the psychopathic sex-killer of Gloucester, has rather queered the pitch.

James works because it's fine by itself and equally handy as Jamie or Jim. Michael doesn't give too many games away, and Mike Thomas is definitely a clean-cut, slightly boring sort of bloke about whom no one need feel embarrassed. Paul Thomas is good, as is Charlie Thomas. Oh, stuff it, I'd have stuck to David and have done.

With girls, it is both easier ... and more difficult. The good news is that the implications of girls' names are less devastating. Just as they can be tomboys, or girlies, or both, or neither, they can stand a wider variation of names without their gender-identity collapsing.

Some friends of mine, briefly obsessed by the belief that you could raise children outside conventional sex-role stereotypes, called their first child Alex, because it was gender-neutral: short for both Alexander or Alexandra. Actually, what it is is a boy's name. But girls can have boys' names, just like they can wear boys' clothes. As Johnny Cash has observed, you can't call a boy Sue, any more than you can put his hair in bunches, or send him off to school in a frock. When the couple had their second child they called him Joe. Another neutral name, they said. Another boy, say I.

We, though, faced a different problem. Taking the view that it was sexist to presume that there was something inherently inferior about a patently feminine name (well, actually, we couldn't have given a stuff about ideology in this instance, but that was the rationale we gave our friends), we were perfectly happy to call a girl a girl, paint her bedroom pink and bury her in Barbies, if that's what she wanted.

But if we gave a daughter a simple name, like Mary, Jane or Kate, the end result would just be nondescript. Mary Thomas. Jane Thomas, Kate Thomas. Nice ... but dull. That, of course, was exactly the effect we were aiming for in a boy – the nominal equivalent of a well-cut suit that reveals nothing whatsoever of the man inside – but it wouldn't work for a girl. A girl needs something more, like the beautiful dress that flatters and presents her figure. And yes, I know this is all sounding very old-fashioned, but it's amazing how archaic you become when it's your children that are on the line.

And just to stretch the clothing metaphor a little bit further, the difficulty with girls' names is that you're spoiled for choice. Boys' names are as restricted as their apparel, but that does at least simplify things somewhat. For girls, the lack of limitations becomes its own problem. That's why it's so difficult for women to decide what to wear: there's just too damn much to choose from. We put on our trousers, shirts, jackets, ties, shoes. They have to think about shapes, hemlines, heels, tights, jewellery. Then they have to take it all off because their bum looks too big. Then they decide it didn't after all. Choice … it's exhausting.

It's the same thing with names. We couldn't go for minimal and plain, but if we went the frou-frou route that was just as bad. My girlfriend Iona had a sister called Arabella. Now, say what you like about the name Arabella Stormonth-Darling, but you have to admit that it's all of a piece. It screams gravel drives and big hats and the Royal Enclosure at Ascot. But, to my way of thinking, Arabella Thomas was like a council house with a bloody great Georgian portico tacked on the front. The two halves just didn't match. And the same went for any other obviously fancy name – Henrietta, Araminta, all that sort of thing.

Looking back, I have to say that Arabella Thomas seems like quite a charming name, particularly when you think that it could have been shortened to Bella. But what if Bella Thomas wasn't very bella, after all? You see, it's just too risky. And note, too, the to-ing and fro-ing, the bursts of enthusiasm and rapid changes of mind: that's what it's like when you're trying to name the lump that's expanding, almost before your eyes, inside your partner's tummy.

We went through endless lists and permutations. We spoke to friends and family. We begged and grovelled for advice. And then, lying on the sofa one day, flicking through one of those books of names you get from Smith's, I saw Holly. And I stopped. I thought of Holly Golightly, and Audrey Hepburn, my all-time favourite cinematic goddess. Then I thought, Holly Thomas. It was a bright, friendly sort of name. It scanned nicely, was easy to say and remember. It was neither dull, nor pretentious and revealed nothing of class or background. It was fresh and original. And, as an added bonus, it would, I reckoned, make a splendid newspaper by-line.

I asked Clare what she thought. She liked Holly, too. And suddenly the problem was solved. We threw away the name books, stopped the conversations. The deal was done. Annoyingly, it looks as though we weren't the only people to come to the same conclusion, because

Holly – though still quite rare – is becoming more popular, but then, you can't have everything.

When Holly was born we gave her two more names: Miranda, in case she thought Holly was too childish when she grew up, which I now very much doubt, and Clare, after her mum. When a second girl came along, just eighteen months later, we toyed for a micro-second with Ivy, considered Violet (my dear grandmother's name) and settled on Lucy – a lot more common than Holly, but sweet just the same.

Looking back, it's hard to imagine how the two of them could have been called anything else. But then, even the most unlikely names are like that in retrospect. I mean, who would ever call a group the Beatles, which is clearly a wet, feeble name, or let a boy like Bruce Springsteen start a musical career without getting him to switch to something less cumbersome?

Still, there's no avoiding the agonies of name selection. As I write these words, my brother and sister-in-law have just produced a daughter. When she was born, they decided to christen her Leila. But when the new mother told her father, he went off the deep end. No grandchild of his was going to be given a Palestinian name. It was inconceivable. No.

The first I knew of it was when we got a card saying that the girl was now to be called Natasha, and assuring us that this was positively the last change that was going to be made. Except it wasn't. A week or so later, the couple and their new-born babe came to visit us in the country. They spent much of their time arguing furiously. He was damned if he was going to change his daughter's name again. She wasn't happy with Natasha any more.

As of now, the child is called Suzannah. As of now, my brother and sister-in-law are still married. By the time you read these words, both those situations may have changed. So it's a pity my feuding family have forgotten that most clichéd of Shakespearean quotes: the one about a rose by any other name smelling as sweet. Because the silly thing is, no matter what you call your kids, you love them just the same. Assuming you love them at all, that is. And if you don't, the name is immaterial anyway.

Rob Ryan

Rob Ryan was born in Liverpool
but, unable to master the tricky
accent or decide whether it was
expedient to support Liverpool or
Everton, he was forced to seek
his fortune in London. He spent
several years as a biology lecturer
before being saved by *The Face*
and, subsequently, *Arena*, for
which he is contributing editor.
He is currently deputy travel
editor on the *Sunday Times*.
His daughter Bella was born
on 27 December 1992; his
second, Gina, arrived in the
kitchen on 30 June 1996.

Welcome to the Pleasuredome

Rob Ryan celebrates sex
and pregnancy

When my wife first announced her pregnancy, I admit it was only my second or third thought: it certainly came after the one about having to pay the mortgage on a single income. But it did pop up, from that little devil on my left shoulder. While the angel on the right was cooing reassuring sounds about me not shooting blanks after all, and contributing a little part of me to the great gene pool of eternity, the devil amid the dandruff was speculating on the impending collapse of both my social and my sex life.

I must admit I had never given the post-conception version of the latter too much thought. References to it in the public domain seemed few and far between. I did recall an interview with the ageing satyrette Roman Polanski, where he claimed that during Sharon Tate's pregnancy he never made love to her. His reasoning was simple and blunt: he didn't have to because there were always other women available. Thanks, Roman, that is a great help.

Then there was Robin Williams' routine about one of the great ironies of pregnancy: your wife suddenly gets a Pammy-style bosom, but declares 'they're for BABY'. It was when the 'Titty Fairy', as he christened the remarkable process of cups running over, actually arrived for us that I realized some of these preconceptions were wrong.

They may be earmarked for the baby, but for several months you – or at least I did, Robin – have Access All Areas visiting rights. Polanski didn't know what he was missing: most pregnant women, just prior to turning into milchcows, become some kind of sex machine.

I had assumed my wife's thoughts would turn to nursery colours, whether to use terries or disposables, if she should opt for an epidural. What I didn't realize was that the first sign of a tumescent tummy also signals the start of a voracious carnality. I am not sure whether Neil Young is right and welfare mothers make better lovers, but freshly pregnant ones take some beating.

I had expected every other symptom: the lethargy, the morning sickness, the quirky food cravings, even the fascism of the National Childbirth Trust classes (any form of drugs = bad, failed mother), but nobody – and especially not any of the expectant-father books – warned me that morning sickness is followed by morning libidity, where a woman made powerful by a heady cocktail of hormones and a vastly increased red cell count throws you on your back and demands pleasure. By hook or by crook, bribery or coercion, flattery or ridicule, you *will* perform. And before you go down to make the tea, to boot.

I can't be the only man ever to be perplexed (and, yes, pleasantly surprised on occasion) by this. I was well aware of the whole madonna/whore complex, the supposed dichotomy between a man's desire in the bedroom and the kitchen, I just was not aware that, like some odd variation of *Invasion of the Body Snatchers*, it was temporally possible for these two to cohabit the same body simultaneously. I know there have been a few trailblazers here, pointing out that pregnancy and sexuality often go hand in hand – Demi Moore in *Vanity Fair*, a hugely gravid Neneh Cherry on *Top of the Pops*, and those Italian strippers who double their money when pregnant – but a little more overt warning – such as, join that gym now, dad-to-be – would have been nice.

The chemical culprit (or is that hero?) here is probably progesterone. Some men out there may have noticed a little libido flip in their partners close to menstruation. This is supposed to be due to the hormone progesterone, which peaks just prior to the blood flow. However, if fertilization has occurred its levels stay high, right the way through to the big event. Combine that with increased blood flow to the breasts and heavy vascularization of the pelvic area and – not to be dismissed lightly – the knowledge that contraception is no longer an issue, and you have serious sexual firepower.

It turned out that this phenomenon has been in the literature for years, had I known where to look. Masters and Johnson, the famed behaviourists and sex therapists, catalogued that sexual desire increased between week 15 (after the tiredness/sickness has worn off) and week 28 (when things get physically more difficult). At least that is the M & J theory: my experience (and that of an ad hoc sample of freshly fathering friends) was that the week 28 marker-board flashed by and was ignored. No way were these women coming into the carnal pits: no matter how difficult the process, sex was staying on the menu.

It may be all *9½ Weeks* to begin with, of course, but things get a little trickier at 29½ weeks, and positively impractical at 39½ weeks. By then, of course, it's a case of working around something BIG that has come between you: towards the end of term, the word 'functional' starts to apply. One recent mother told me: 'It was disgusting. I was just so gross.' I tried to assure her it was probably a beautiful, moving thing. 'No,' she said, 'it *was* disgusting because my husband told me so afterwards. But he just gritted his teeth at the time.' At least he knew when to keep his mouth shut.

Even this very late version of sex has a usefulness. Sperm contains potent chemicals called prostaglandins, which help soften the cervix and may initiate delivery. It is not unusual for women with tardy babies to be told to go home and fuck if they want to get things moving. There are also theories that the biological imperative for an orgasm in this situation helps exercise a few of the muscles that will be involved in passing what is effectively a small melon down the birth canal.

My survey also found a few misgivings among both sexes about the whole process, because, well, sex is no longer a beautiful thing just between the two of you. There is a third party, unseen, yet a silent witness to the whole event. Early on, of course, you can ignore what lies at the end of the vaginal tube, forget that this is troilism-with-a-foetus. Later, it may dominate the whole procedure.

'I could not help feeling it was, you know, going to get a face full,' said one friend. Biologically impossible, but just knowing it is up there can have a detrimental effect on performance, let alone when it makes its presence felt: 'It was all OK,' said one male friend, 'until right at the end when you could see ripples and movement on the stomach. I kept thinking about John Hurt, and all at once everything would go soft. It was like trying to put a marshmallow into a parking meter.' Now there is a man without imagination – if he had thought of Ripley rather than ripples he might have got somewhere.

My own problem was not with the actual sex before birth but –

just to prove that you can read too much – the theories of a Frenchman who predicted dire consequences for our subsequent sexual profile if I allowed myself to witness the actual birth.

Now I must admit that a bit of contrariness had already entered my head over this whole husband-at-birth thing. Far from being there with a camcorder, I rather fancied a return to the traditional male role of pacing outside the delivery room, a pocketful of fine Cohiba cigars, ordering towels and hot water as necessary. (I finally discovered why they always do that in Westerns: hot salt compresses were once used to help stretch the opening of the vagina, prior to the advent of the more brutal cut-and-stitch approach.)

Part of my reluctance stemmed from a cynicism about the role of men in the delivery process: all the rhetoric about shared pain struck me as a spurious device to make the redundant partner feel involved. I mean, no one ever offers to come to the dentist with you and squeeze your hand and play synchronized rinsing, do they? Cultures where birth is an all-female experience seemed more sensible. (This was prior to the recent theories that being a sharing, caring birth partner helps initiate post-natal depression – an excuse my wife has accused me of over-exploiting during her second pregnancy.)

Then I read that Michel Odent, an influential French obstetrician, had declared that witnessing the event can have catastrophic consequences: 'I am not saying fathers should never be present at birth,' he told one reporter, 'but they can be more trouble than they are worth ... One reason, I believe, why marriages commonly break up soon after childbirth is that all the mystery has gone, there is no sexual attraction any more.' Gulp.

Against this doom-mongering I had to stack those male friends who had claimed the experience as the most moving of their lives and dismissed Odent's views as the rantings of a maverick. Odent, incidentally, is on record as saying it is OK for men to have mistresses while their wives are breastfeeding, because they are not attractive during this phase, and their sexual activity is low. Very pragmatic; very Gallic. My wife Deborah and I decided on a compromise that would put me in the room, but might save our marriage: I would be present but so would Deborah's mother, who, after all, had more of an inkling of what it would feel like than I ever could, plus the qualified midwife who served the area. But just in case Odent had a point, Deborah insisted: 'I want you up at the head end, not down there tugging the baby out.' It was all I could do to resist insisting she put that in writing.

Our planned all-natural 100 per cent wholewheat water-birth-with-soft-music-and-incense totally collapsed and, after three days of laborious and futile home labour, we found ourselves in a ward straight out of the Roswell incident, filled with bright lights and an anonymous gynaecological SWAT team who had descended on us: two doctors, a second midwife, a paediatrician and all kinds of resuscitating equipment, just in case. Eventually, when the baby started to show signs of distress, the doctor decided to go in there and pull the poor thing out with those overgrown sugar tongs they keep hidden from you. The thought spurred Deborah on, and the doc suddenly shouted to me, 'I can see the head. Do you want to look?'

I heard the words of Michel Odent echoing round my head. Look down there, *mon brave*, and your sexual world may fall apart; every time you do it, it will feel like you are trying to get back into the womb the hard way. I turned to Deborah. Let her decide: I could always use it in arguments later.

'Do I want to look?' She nodded, and I glimpsed a tiny patch of scalp awaiting entry to the world. 'What colour is it?' asked Deborah. Dumbfounded, I could only say, 'White. What colour were you expecting?'

'The hair, you idiot. What colour is the hair?'

And so at 3.35 p.m., 27 December 1992, the baby was gently levered into this life with the sound of slightly hysterical laughter ringing in her ears. To paraphrase Dorothy Parker, although I knew Deborah had it in her, I didn't truly believe we were going to have a baby until it slithered out, an eight-pound two-ounce patchwork of shocking pink and greenish slime. And I have to admit, sex wasn't on either of our minds just then.

So what about the mistress thing while breastfeeding? Not, believe me, an option here. But it is true that sexual desire for most women takes a bit of a holiday. And even if it didn't, things tend to be somewhat messy for a while. One couple we met at NCT classes, who ate part of the placenta fried with champagne, later claimed to have had sex within two days of delivery, although I was forced to tell the husband that intercourse with the placenta leftovers didn't actually count. Funny, we never did keep in touch.

Even when the healing process is well under way, there are some fresh barriers to breach. There may be stitches and therefore scar tissue, which the mother will be convinced feels like the internal tyre marks of some giant earthmover. Be reassuring: say they are but the imprint of a Dinky toy version of an earthmover. Or something. (I went for the 'Scar, what scar?' approach.)

But there is also the vexed problem of breasts. Now they really are for the baby. And although some fine young cannibals probably incorporate lactation into the sexual act, personally I have a problem with that. So you have to readjust your sights, and your foreplay, a little. You quickly learn to work around them. And, if things get messy, just remember that little euphemism that Universal Studios use when someone has been queasy on one of their rides: 'Uh-oh, I think we have a protein spill here.' Mind you, a protein spill of sorts got you into this mess in the first place.

Trickiest of all is the whole question of size. Don't even joke about this. You wouldn't like to be told you had a prick like a reject chipolata; so sausage-up-an-alley comments, even in jest, are out. If she asks can you feel the sides, don't say 'Yes. Well, side, anyway'. The human body is remarkably elastic: it's just that this particular rubber band snaps back in very slow motion.

So it is no surprise that psychologically and physically the first sex since birth is supposed to be the big barrier. But there is one enormous spur to doing it (or to lying). Come the first serious post-natal check-up at six weeks the midwife is going to ask if husband and wife have resumed sexual relations. No problem if you haven't, they assure you, but you can't help feeling this is something of a test. For the record, we made it. By twenty-four hours. There was no way my wife was going to have a 'No', or a 'Not yet' or an 'Any day now' next to that question, stitches and leaking breasts be damned.

Stephen Amidon

Stephen Amidon was born in
Chicago. He is the author of
four works of fiction,
the most recent of which is
The Primitive (Gollancz).
He has written extensively for
Esquire and the *Sunday Times*.
He currently lives in London
with his wife Caryl and their
two children, Clementine and
Alexander, who caused lots of
trouble getting here but have
been angels ever since.

The Delivery

Stephen Amidon is there

After eighteen hours they start talking about the blade. I'm not sure who brings it up first, just that this rumour of a knife now circulates through the delivery room like a cloud of invisible but noxious gas. Maybe it was the chief midwife, the one with the studded ears and grim mouth, who first mentioned the possibility. Or perhaps it was the tall doctor leaning against the door jamb, examining my wife's distended belly as if it were a Sunday roast ready for the carving. Or maybe it was the anaesthetist, fiddling with the IV drip that hangs above us all like the udder of some long-legged beast.

Whoever first brought it up, there is no denying that the possibility of my wife being sliced open is now among us, as big and bad and unavoidable as the proverbial 800-pound gorilla in your living room. What's more, it is becoming clear that, no matter who asked the question, there is only one person currently expected to answer it. Not Caryl, who, after three-quarters of a day being pounded by an internal gale, wants only for the storm to be over. Not any of the three midwives in the room, who seem to be tripping over each other to avoid my eye. The gas-passer, meanwhile, is making it clear that it's all the same to her if we cut or not, while the obstetrician, whose call you'd think it should be, has yet even to set foot in the room. And the awestruck student shrinking into the furthest possible corner seems incapable of deciding whether or not to take her next breath.

No. None of these people want to make the decision. It's up to me.

So, after hours of more or less non-stop uselessness, I suddenly find myself thrust centre stage, a position for which I am not even remotely prepared. So I do what comes natural. I balk. I freeze. If only there weren't so many people in the room, is all I can think. It's like the cabin scene from *A Night at the Opera* in here. There are a half-dozen of these strangers in all, none of them particularly interested in Caryl, whose eyes are now shut as she travels through some internal, infernal landscape of pain. If only they would go, then maybe I could think, maybe I could figure out what to do.

But no one is going anywhere. In fact, after noting my indecision they all lapse into a medical lingo that I don't speak. To my horror, I realize that if I don't say something now my silence will be taken as assent. I will have given the nod to the one thing my wife wants to avoid, if at all possible. The Caesarean Section.

'Excuse me,' I mutter from my bed-side post. 'Uh, people?'

I am ignored. The butch midwife and the doctor are well into their interventionist plans. The gas-passer joins them, a narcotic gleam in her eye. Watches are checked. The student is looking at me and Caryl with open pity. The decision, it seems, has already been made.

No, I think. Don't let this happen. Not yet. And then, something in me gives. A boundary of civility and deference is crossed. Adrenalized blood rushes to my head.

'Listen up!' I say, one decibel below shouting volume.

Everything stops. Even my wife's umpteenth contraction seems to undergo a brief caesura. All eyes are on me.

'You and you and you and you and you – out!'

The butch midwife and her assistants and the student and the anaesthetist look at me with slack-jawed wonder.

'And you,' I'm pointing at the doctor now. 'Take a walk. I want to talk to my wife for a minute.'

To my complete and utter amazement, it works. The midwives disappear. The gas-passer makes a final adjustment and slinks off. The student might not have even been here. And, to my astonished relief, the gimlet-eyed doctor mutters something about giving us a while, then strolls off down the hall in his cushioned shoes.

I look back at my wife.

'Hey, Caryl?'

We are having our first baby. Check that. Caryl is having *her* first baby. That quaint plural pronoun, I am discovering, was discarded the moment the first contraction rolled in like a tsunami in an Irwin Allen film. Chucked out along with those much-maligned breathing exercises and the bold interdictions against the use of anaesthetics. Where labour starts, *we* stops. Sure, we made the love that got us into this mess. We gripped that shared phone when announcing the pregnancy to our families. We went for ceremonial curries after the antenatal classes each Thursday night.

But *she* is having the kid.

It all starts according to plan. The contractions roll in on the exact due date, 22 October, commencing just as the bell tolls for the six o'clock news. At first we think they are just another vivid spell of phantom Braxton-Hicks contractions. You know Messrs Braxton and Hicks, that vaudevillian comedy team of the delivery process whose schtick is to lull you into a false sense of security about the real thing, making you believe that when labour actually arrives it will be manageable, nothing more than a rather aggravated flutter below the solar plexus. But then Caryl bounces off the sofa as if she's been jolted by Sensurround.

'I think this is it,' she says in an eerily faraway voice.

We call the hospital. They tell us to take it easy. Just behave normally, whatever that may be. So we enter a bizarre simulacrum of an evening at home. Only we cannot eat or drink anything except water. We can't go out to the pub or take in a film. There's nothing on television and a walk is out of the question. The only thing we can do is not go to the hospital. Not yet. Caryl takes a supposedly soothing bath, though it soon becomes clear that the contractions are coming with increasing vigour. I make a mess of timing the intervals. They are either two minutes apart or eighteen seconds.

And then, less than three hours after the process begins, I do the one thing I have promised myself I wouldn't do. I panic. I lose it. No, I don't start running around like Jerry Lewis. I don't faint, nor do I decide I want to be single again. It is more subtle than that. I simply ask a question, sow a seed of doubt in Caryl's hormonally charged mind, which soon blossoms into a full-blown Chinese fire drill.

'Do you think maybe we should head on over to the hospital?' I muse. 'I mean, didn't your mom have like a, what, two-hour labour or something?'

Twenty-four minutes later a cadaverous porter ushers us through the gothic halls of the West London Hospital, since boarded up after a malignant vein of asbestos was discovered percolating in its yellowy walls. I look around. So here we finally are, at the maternity hospital, that New Age Bedlam where nobody is sick and yet everybody's hurting, where people are doing the sanest thing possible and yet everybody's crazy. After riding up in what appears to be the same elevator Anjelica Huston descended in at the end of *The Grifters*, we are led to a delivery room.

Our midwife arrives a few moments later, an officious and exhausted middle-aged woman whose name I never do get. The first thing she does is hook Caryl up to a monitor which provides numerical proof that actual contractions are occurring, a sort of rolling Richter scale of the seismic activity in the fault line below her navel. This is good. Numbers. Data. Not me with a stopwatch, but digits pulsing with red authority on the LED meter. Eight years on I don't remember the numerical range, just that the analytical, problemsolving part of my mind finally had a graph to climb and parameters to maintain. For the first time since Caryl began to blow, I feel on solid ground.

The midwife seems impressed by the numbers. They're big. Fat with pain and promise. Which can mean only one thing – zero hour is close at hand. Unfortunately, there is one other number to deal with before we can get the show on the road. Cervical dilation. I know from the Thursday night classes that we are aiming for a perfect ten centimetres. But the midwife informs us that after over four hours of strenuous effort we are still at nil. Zip. Goose egg. Not even on the chart. I feel like a basketball coach who is forced to call time out when his team goes down 12–0 after two minutes of play.

The midwife snaps off her latex gloves and informs me that, in principle, we shouldn't actually be in hospital yet. But we are. Caryl is looking at me from the bed. This is it. The dreaded moment. I have to make my first executive decision of the evening. Not fobbing it off on Caryl like I did back at the flat. I stall by asking the midwife for a rundown of our options. There are exactly two. Caryl can either be shipped off to a ward to try to get a night's sleep amid thirty squirming, mewling, coughing strangers (and no me), or we can head home. What we cannot do is stay in the delivery room with its reassuring array of equipment that purrs and hums with the sibilant authority of relief. That is needed for somebody with a more pliant cervix than we have to offer.

The midwife wants to keep Caryl in the hospital. My wife, hardly surprisingly, opts for home. There's a pause and then I make the call. Home it is. I don't want to cross Caryl, not yet. The power structure around here hints that there may be a need to do that in a big way later.

We drive back through the sodium-lit streets of west London. It is 1 a.m. Caryl takes another bath. I flip on the tube but this is 1988, back when the British still believed that people should stop watching television at midnight and get some shut-eye. Improbably, all I can find is a rerun of an American college football game on ITV, two Midwestern behemoths slugging it out for the conference crown. Suffering no doubt from some deep stress trauma, I find myself engrossed in whether or not the Oklahoma Sooners will get the ball back for one last shot at glory. That is, until Caryl calls from the bathroom. 'What the fuck are you doing in there? Are you watching *sport*?'

I go to the door. Caryl is in serious agony, twisting in the tub like one of those Japanese victims of mercury poisoning. Our eyes meet. Though nothing is said, a dawning realization passes between us that the pre-fight hype about this being a manageable process has just flown out the window. In the hormonal lottery that gives some women relatively swift labours and others Burma death marches towards torture chambers filled with forceps and scalpels, we've drawn the short stick. There, in that steamy room, we both acknowledge something we hadn't banked on. We're in for the long haul. I sneak a look at my watch. It's 3.33 a.m.

'Can I make you some tea?'

But she doesn't answer. Another contraction has just arrived.

We are back at the hospital well before dawn to be met by the same lugubrious porter wheeling the same rickety chair. I flash him a self-deprecating 'us again' smile but he merely deadpans back, clearly zombified by years of serving as Charon to countless pumped-up, terrified couples on their way into the Stygian gloom of labour. There's something eerily cautionary about his dour countenance, a reminder that we are not Mr and Mrs Special after all, but rather just more specimens trundling along a mercilessly non-stop biological assembly line.

We ascend in the same caged elevator, though this time we are led to a different room. There's been a shift change, thank God, and we have a new midwife. Janet. Middle-aged, black, her Caribbean voice both strong and soothing. An authority figure straight out of blissful childhood.

Caryl is hooked back up to the Belly-Richter, which registers numbers that would flatten entire regions of the former Soviet Union. Then the all-important dilation is checked. Janet's poker face betrays a momentary confusion. She shakes her head. Zero-point-five. Not even a single whole digit! Fuck. Five per cent. I do some rough calculation to see how long is left, multiplying the time Caryl has been in labour by twenty and coming up with … no. No way. Surely that isn't possible. Nobody can go through what my wife is now enduring for *that* long. I quell a brief, foreboding glimpse of Caesarean future and turn my attention back to Caryl, who at least seems to be drawing some relief from finally being in the last room where she'll ever experience this sort of pain.

We hope.

We settle in, if that's the phrase for it. For the next two hours we do all the things they told us to do. We breathe, we count, we gobble little slivers of ice. Turf-conscious male that I am, I find myself staking out a patch of linoleum near the upper right-hand corner of the bed, where I can be both close to the action and out of the way. This is the spot they don't tell you about in the classes. Just about the worst location on earth. The Partner's Place. That square yard of neutral ground where you can do little more than stand at frustrated attention, like some ceremonial guard outside a ransacked palace.

We muddle through until dawn happens somewhere out there on the Broadway. Then the next big issue arises. After more than twelve hours, Caryl's astonishing stoicism is starting to falter. Pain relief will be needed if she's to be lucid at the end of the day. Now my attitude towards this matter is, and always has been, simple. Nuke 'em. Hit the suckers with everything you've got – Tomahawks, ICBMs, Polaris-based MIRVs. Bounce the rubble. Then send in the Marines to mop up. Any emanation of pain should be rigorously, mercilessly extirpated using the latest in pharmacological weaponry. Caryl, on the other hand, has always wanted to get through the process without any artificial help. A proud, strong woman, she also has an inbred distrust of doctors and organized medicine that makes the prospect of having her body violated by needles and knives a recurring nightmare.

Janet, who has seen it all and then some, recommends we leap-frog the small arms in the pain war, the nitrous oxide and pethedine, and go right for the baddest of all pain killers. The Big E. The epidural. The vaunted, dreaded spinal block. I look at Caryl, who is undergoing the most vivid of dialectics. On the one hand is her feeling that this would constitute a failure of nerve, as well as those perfectly understandable reservations about having a needle stuck into her spinal column. On the other hand is the fact that Mike Tyson seems to have snuck into the room and is currently rabbit-punching her against the ropes.

It's time for executive decision number two on my part. It's a no-brainer, really. But I cannot simply tell Caryl she has to have her longest bone punctured, that she has to lend the lower half of her body to medical science without any guarantee they'll return it in working order. Instead, I just shrug and assume a what-the-hell manner.

'You know what?' I say. 'You've already been doing this for, like, twelve hours.'

'Thirteen hours and eight minutes.'

'Exactly. The point is, basically, you've been through labour. So why don't you take the epidural? I mean, you've done what you had to. Let Wellcome do the rest.'

Caryl sees right through this gambit but, exhausted, agrees anyway. My pride in having swung matters into the court of modern medicine is soon undercut, however, by the arrival of an exhausted resident anaesthetist, who seems barely out of his teens and has clearly just been dragged from some major REM action. It takes him a long time to find the right spot in Caryl's spine. I am tempted to say that muttering 'damn' is probably not the best bedside manner but don't want to get into it with him. Not while he has a sharp object in my wife's back.

Finally, he manages to pin the tail on the patient and leaves, yawning and bleary-eyed.

'Feeling better?' I ask Caryl.

'Sort of.'

Morning proceeds. At first, the spinal block seems to work its reputed wonders – Caryl has a pain-free hour. But our reprieve is short-lived. The hurt returns, far too quickly. And not only that, but it is now located solely on the right side of her body. I bring the matter to Janet's attention, who looks dubious and indicates we'll just have to tough it out until the next top-up in a few hours. I look at Caryl, who is distraught by the news. We have come too close to pain-freedom to be plunged back into the abyss.

I grow momentarily furious. Janet and I have gotten along just fine until now – I've stayed amiable and quiet in my Partner's Place. I take a few deep breaths before responding. After all, I don't want to fly off the handle, especially in a radically midwife-oriented hospital where doctors have to be invited into the delivery room. And the fact that I, a white thirty-year-old middle-class American am squaring off with a black fifty-year-old in close quarters *on her turf*, further complicates matters. There are power issues here which I don't have a clue about how to resolve.

I take a few more deep breaths and realize that all that in-out lung training serves a purpose after all. It allows the partner to keep from losing his shit.

'Maybe we can wake up Dr Sleepy just to have a look?' I suggest, artfully displacing my anger on the absent party.

Janet agrees. Thank God. The anaesthetist is summoned and, to my relief, a different doctor arrives, a plump, no-nonsense woman on the cusp of her shift. After a cursory examination she discovers that the previous gas-passer had made a meal of the epidural – the needle hangs out of Caryl's lumbar region like a poorly tossed dart. She's getting less than 50 per cent of the drugs she needs. The rest is seeping into her tissue like water from a leaky hose. For a moment I lament the fact that we are not back in my native land – the malpractice settlement would send my forthcoming kid to an Ivy League school and beyond.

It becomes clear, however, that no damage has been done. Caryl's spine is soon as thickly blocked as the Broadway. Dilation is still disappointingly sparse, but at least welcome respite is at hand. Caryl manages a weak smile and, amazingly, expresses concern about how ragged I look. After sixteen hours on my feet, I am excused for lunch.

I find a kebab place that looks like a training ground for health inspectors but promises to get a maximum amount of protein into my guts in the shortest possible time. As I tear recklessly into the starch and gristle, I begin to think about my father. As with nearly all men of his generation, his non-participation in the births of his children is legendary. Word is that he was watching *The Three Stooges* in a waiting room when I moled my way to earth. And I remember being taken as a six-year-old to a field adjacent to a hospital to view my sister, held aloft behind the ward's second-storey window, as if the presence of her father and brothers were a potential contaminant.

For the first time, I begin to understand that generation's acquiescence to this banishment. The men could have been there if they wanted. They just didn't want. And it wasn't about squeamishness or sterility, either. Nor was it about lack of concern – these guys broke their backs and ruptured their guts constructing safe familial havens. No, I think it was about power, about a reluctance to step into a place where their every instinct would tell them to take charge, to sort things out and stop all this hurting. An instinct that they would be largely powerless to act upon. Just as I was now discovering. So, they decided, the hell with it. Leave it to the pros. Walk the halls, make some calls. Be anywhere but in that place by the head of the bed, that biological penalty box where you have to sit still and watch your team getting hammered.

The place it is just about time to get back to.

After I return, things start to go from bad to worse. There's been a shift change and Janet has been replaced by Nora, the nice but passive midwife who taught our antenatal classes. What's more, she is joined by two no-nonsense colleagues, including her man-hating shift commander. Although Caryl's pain is no longer acute, her body's unwillingness to speed things up is starting to exhaust her. The fear is that when the push/don't push routine arrives she simply won't have the energy to perform.

It is this dilemma that brings on the Caesarean crisis. It is this that leaves us alone in the room. I wait until the current spell of contractions has ended and then speak Caryl's name a second time. She opens her eyes. I don't have to explain. She's no dummy. She knows what's going on. Right away, I can see the answer. She is not going to be cut. No way. Not now. Not unless somebody uses the phrase 'life-saving'. Until then, we tough it out. Her expression tells me that she knows they're wrong, that she can get through this thing without their bloody intervention.

Nora reappears in the doorway. Sent, no doubt, by her butch boss and the slice-happy doctor.

'We're OK,' I say. 'Tell them we're OK. We'll do this like we planned.'

Nora agrees reluctantly, though she hints the matter might soon be out of our hands. I look back at Caryl. Her eyes fill with relief. For an instant we are transported into an ironic, placid place, beyond all the pain and confusion. For the briefest of moments, we are Stephen and Caryl again, not POWs in some gruesome labour camp, but a strong and confident couple who can deal with pretty much whatever the world dishes out. For the first time in the whole long session I feel truly useful. As if my presence counted for something in this weird, fraught place.

Of course it doesn't last. Nothing lasts in labour. Everything goes away and then comes back again, usually with a vengeance and when you least want it. Especially the pain. Which comes now, unimpressed by my transitory spell of authority.

But then, over the next few minutes, something strange and miraculous starts to happen. As if spurred on by the recent crisis, Caryl's body finally decides to eject this interloper. We start to see some big movement in that pesky cervix – it yawns from three to six centimetres in a half-hour. The drugs wear off and, unbelievably, we enter the mythic push/pant/panic phase. More midwives arrive, though this time their presence is welcome, benign. Everybody dons gloves and gowns. I make myself useful by serving as communications director between the pros down there in mission control and Caryl circling in pain's wobbly orbit.

And then our child's head appears like a moon after a long eclipse.

Now, fatherhood in labour is a condition shrouded in myth. Some of these folk tales, like the sense of utter uselessness, are truer than anyone can imagine. Others, like feelings of squeamishness at the sight of blood and placenta, are bullshit, lore born of ignorance and fear. Truth is, as the birth proceeds, I don't have a nanosecond's sense of disgust for the rather frank display of fluid and tissue. And it's not because I'm a tough guy. In these matters, I'd say I'm about average. No, the reason is much more fundamental. You see, I'm not squeamish because, for those last few minutes of my wife's labour, I'm simply *not there*. From the moment the baby slips into the birth canal until it is weighed, tagged and wrapped, I undergo a transcendental experience that gnarly Himalayans spend lifetimes in search of – I am utterly ego-less, totally unselfconscious. Every photon of my attention is locked on Caryl as she tries to deal with this astonishing, unprecedented occurrence. When a shard of refreshing ice is needed, I am Scott of the Antarctic. When fast and accurate directions have to be given, I am Gene Krantz back in Houston talking to the boys in Apollo 13. When her benumbed leg slips from the gurney, I catch it like Willie Mays settling under an easy pop fly. The one thing I am not is Stephen Amidon, that too-brooding writer given to the unrewarding narcissism his craft often requires. Gone completely is the confusion about my role that has plagued me since the previous evening. And I'll tell you something, it feels good, not feeling anything at all. This, I later realize, is what my father and his generation missed. This glorious release that comes at the end of that dark tunnel of hopelessness. This hour of freedom from the gut-wrenching chore of responsibility. This delivery from the self.

And then, after twenty-two hours in Amityville, it happens. The reason for the delay becomes clear when we discover the child's hand had been resting against its cheek like some foetal Jack Benny, enlarging the head and slowing down the whole damned show. Once this is sorted the baby slides out as smooth and fast as an East German bobsledder. It is a girl and because it is a girl she is Clementine, the name that had come to us like an epiphany while watching the John Ford film just a week earlier. She's an eight-pound one-ounce beauty with a wary, slightly annoyed expression which she still gets to this day when people mess with her. After being passed about the room like a rugby ball she is touched down on her mother's breast.

And then I become Stephen Amidon again. I make sure Caryl has everything she needs before going out to the hall to make the usual calls. As I do I notice that I am being watched by a man whose wife is obviously in the early stages of labour. He has that rookie look about him, the same pre-game jitters I was experiencing twenty-four hours earlier. His eyes are full of envy for the moment when he too can get on the horn and spread the good word. I nod to him, the ageing vet assuring the frightened kid, letting him know I was there once, hours ago, seasons ago.

I reach my folks back in Arizona. My mother hogs the phone but I do get a word in with my father. He asks how Caryl is, how it went. I cannot help but think of him and his Three Stooges, of me and my perfect ego-less moment.

'It was great,' I answer. 'You should have been there.'

Jim McClellan

Jim McClellan lives in Camberwell
and works as a freelance
journalist. He is a contributing
editor to *The Face* and *i-D* and has
written for *Arena, Esquire*, the
Observer, the *Independent* and
Brutus magazine in Japan.
He currently writes a fortnightly
column about the Internet for the
Guardian's Online section. Earlier
this year he realized that he has
now watched *Pingu's Big Video*
more times than *Taxi Driver* and
he suspects this may constitute
some kind of milestone.

No Cigar

Jim McClellan tries to mark the occasion

It would be nice to think that if I'd just smoked a cigar the night my daughter was born, I would have saved myself a lot of trouble. I would have got a number of things – specifically a desire to somehow mark the occasion – out of my system. It would be nice to think that … though I'd probably be kidding myself. An expensively aromatic big boy's smoke is supposed to be the way men mark their transition to fatherhood, at least if you live your life according to pop cultural stereotypes. After the post-coital fag, nine months after to be precise, comes the post-natal cigar. Indeed, I've read magazine columns written by professional stogy chompers who said that fatherhood was what kickstarted their habit.

I certainly had the opportunity to have a quiet reflective smoke. I spent my first night as a father home alone, wondering what to do with myself. I imagine it's not that uncommon an experience if your first child is born in hospital. My girlfriend Kim and our new daughter Lee stayed in St Thomas's, which sits on the other side of the Thames from the Houses of Parliament, though they slept apart. The midwives sensibly took Lee away so that Kim could get some rest. I went back to our flat in Stockwell. I seemed to have come home to some odd kind of interregnum. The baby stuff was there ready and waiting – the Moses basket by the side of the bed, the changing station set up in the corner of our bedroom. But the expected chaos, the crying baby, the open nappy sacks – all that was absent. It seemed like some kind of significant pause, a chance to take stock. A good time, in other words, to smoke 'the cigar'.

Though I didn't smoke and hadn't planned ahead, I thought I had some cigars in the flat – the left-overs of an old stash maintained by my girlfriend's grandfather, a man who knew what he liked and bought in bulk. On visiting his house once, I found the cupboards filled with dozens of neatly stacked packets of Tuc crackers (his favourite late-night nibble) and Tupperware bowls filled with sherbert lemons (his choice of sweet). Though he seemed more of a pipe man when I met him, clearly at some point he had liked his cigars. He still had a tin full of the things, which found its way to me after he died. For a while, I passed them round on nights out with the boys. At the time, in their search for forms of conventional male drag they might ironically try on in order to irritate (or spice things up with) their long-term girlfriends, they had lighted on cigars. Most social occasions were liberally fumigated with whatever slim panatellas happened to be on sale at the bar.

I thought I still had a few left. But I found I'd actually given away pretty much the whole lot. All that remained was a brown-round-the-edges pack of Hamlets. Knowing my girlfriend's grandfather, it was quite possible he'd bought these at some point in the sixties. Would they be OK? Did cigars go off or did they get better with age? Were Hamlets any good? I didn't know. However, I did remember the Hamlet ad campaign, in which they figured as small consolations for comical cock-ups. This didn't seem quite the flavour I was after. I spent a while wondering what sort of cigars the late-night place down the road would sell. Then, in a foreshadowing of the infinitely fatigued shape of things to come, when contact with alcohol, no matter how small the amount, would render me instantly comatose, I drank a bottle of cheap French lager and fell fast asleep on the sofa.

New dads are probably the easiest of easy marks. If they haven't sorted it already, the double-glazing salesmen of the world should set up some sort of post-natal bush telegraph to tip each other off as another poor sucker wanders pie-eyed and smiling out of the delivery room. Luckily, I was too busy learning new 'parenting skills' (nappy changing, vomit ducking etc.) to get out of the house much. Otherwise I'm sure I would have come back in a second-hand Skoda

('Nice colour, don't you think?') with a handful of timeshare certificates ('The guy selling them seemed like a nice bloke.') and a copy of that last David Bowie album ('Apparently he's back on form.').

Even at home though, I wasn't out of danger. One Sunday, still basking in the afterglow of it all, I managed to sell myself on the idea of a christening. Kim had been talking on the phone to her sister Philippa, who'd also had a baby daughter, Lydia, six weeks before Lee arrived. She was having her christened. Why not tag along? Kim and Phil's grandmother, now in her eighties, would get to see her great-grandchildren together. It would be a chance for my family to meet Kim's family – something which, since we'd never married, hadn't actually happened. It would be a good excuse for a party. I found it hard to disagree.

On the face of it, it isn't the kind of decision that should excite too much comment. 'Parents to Get Daughter Christened' is the kind of headline which would struggle for space even in the direst local freesheet. Except that for me, splashing a bit of water over a baby's head represented a significant change of heart. It felt like a personal policy U-turn roughly equivalent to Mrs Thatcher deciding that perhaps the miners might have a point after all. For the last twenty years or so, I've generally managed to avoid churches and shunned the company of grown men and women who require you to call them Brother, Sister or, worst of all, Father. I'm happy enough to drop by as a tourist, admire the stained glass, buy a postcard or two. But you don't catch me there on official business.

I was quite devout as a child, though I didn't really have much choice. Born Catholic, I went to a Catholic primary school and, for a couple of years, a Catholic comprehensive. Then, like most people, I let it all go somewhere on the way through adolescence. It was nothing dramatic. I lapsed in slow motion. But by fifteen, I had decided I didn't really believe in God. I still don't. It's not really a big deal. I'm not one of those high and mighty Richard Dawkins God-botherers who feel the need to tell believers they are deluded imbeciles. I'm a sort of quiet atheist, happily secular. Religion, certainly organized religion, wasn't part of my life – that was one of the reasons Kim and I had never married. I didn't need the church. At least, I thought I didn't. So why was I heading back there now?

In my defence, I can say that I wasn't thinking particularly clearly at the time. That contact high that kicks in in the delivery room as you hold that wriggling bundle of new life in your arms hadn't quite gone. By nature something of a grump, I was transformed by Lee's birth into one of the shiny, happy people. And I wanted everyone else to be happy too. So when the subject came up, well, it just seemed like a nice idea. Joint christening? Hell, why not? But aren't you an atheist with little or no time for organized religion? Minor points. This course of action marks me out as a total hypocrite, you say? Relax, it'll be … uh, you know, kind of nice.

It wasn't a help that the christening conversation happened shortly after we'd fulfilled our legal requirements as far as marking Lee's arrival was concerned. One October morning, when Lee was about a month old, we walked down to Brixton Register Office to get her birth certificate. Outside, it was a fairly typical nineties inner-London scene – slightly rundown Victorian terrace surrounded by fast-food joints and all-night supermarkets, with a heavily fortified police station just across the road. Inside, it was as if you had gone through some kind of time warp. Both moulderingly claustrophobic and echoingly empty, the place made the hotel in *Barton Fink* look like the Ritz.

Following a track worn into the dusty shag-pile, we crossed a small waiting room decorated with public information posters dating from the Attlee government, rang a bell and waited until someone surfaced from within. She was perfectly pleasant, helped us through the technicalities. We're not married, wanted both our surnames on the certificate, but not in some kind of tongue-tripping double-barrel. So it was sorted out. We signed on the dotted line and went home. That was it. It was probably the flat bureaucratic emptiness of this that finally softened me up, that made me say yes at the end of the christening conversation.

By then, I had convinced myself that a solo stogy wouldn't have really been enough anyway. I wanted some sort of social event, something collective. If it had to be a cigar, I'd prefer to meet my buddies down the pub, have one hand me something expensively Cuban and impressively lengthy, slapping me on the back in the process, while someone else leaned in with the Zippo. There were two things wrong with this picture. First, I was pretty sure that by now my friends were over their cigar phase. Second, the whole picture sounded like a hokey fashion-spread from a dodgy American men's magazine into ironically repackaging the mores of old-style masculinity.

In fact, the whole cigar thing belongs in the past, somewhere in fifties suburbia. When you think of it, you think of a nervy fresh-faced twenty-ish exec dad, tie loosened, sack suit jacket slung over his shoulder, pacing nervously in hospital waiting rooms. You think of family and friends in attendance, crowding round to congratulate when the all-clear is bawled out in the delivery room. You think of a world in which women are inside the delivery room, ministered to by medical professionals, and men are outside, helped through the whole thing by their family; a world in which women wind up holding the baby and men get to brandish a phallic totem. Now, some people do still live in that world, but you mostly encounter them in sitcoms. It's only on American TV shows like *Friends* that your buddies and any stray family members in the area show up at the hospital as your sprog is about to be dropped. It's only Del Boy that gets to brandish the old tobacco torpedo outside the delivery room. In the real world there are probably by-laws against using any form of nicotine-based product within a half-mile radius of a new-born child.

I couldn't imagine ringing my friends and telling them that things were moving and they'd better get down to St Thomas's. They had jobs to do, daytime TV to watch. My family was scattered across the country and Europe, but even if they had been around, it would have been odd to have them along for the ride. What would they have done? Mill about in the ground-floor shopping mall at St Thomas's? The fact was, not to be cruel or anything but ... I didn't actually need their company. I didn't need to be helped through the long nervous wait. I was busy.

These days, childbirth, especially the actual delivery, is not so much a family affair as a couples thing. Men are supposed to be in there with their wives or girlfriends. They are partners in the whole process. They're supposed to help – do breathing exercises, whisper comforting words, get shouted at. In my case, I spent the time fooling around with a TENS machine. Designed to stimulate the natural production of endorphines (the body's internal aspirin), this is a form of non-drug-based pain relief. In other words, it's pain relief which doesn't work. But at least trying to get it to work kept me busy. I was certainly way too busy to hang with my buddies shooting the breeze over a Corona Grande.

When I did finally meet the boys for a drink after Lee's birth, the idea came up that, rather than smoke a cigar, I should buy a ring. Towards the bleary end of the evening, conversation turned, only somewhat jokily, to the subject of the stereotypical Jamaican baby-father as a possible future paternal role model. Here was someone who wasn't pinned down by all that nuclear 2.2 family values bollocks – that seemed to be the party line. 'Women don't really want men around that much where kids are concerned. They just get in the way. Lots of women these days, they're much happier running things themselves, and anyway it's not as if you abandon your kids. I mean, you're around, but you're not like,"Dad". What babyfathers do, when they have a kid, is buy a ring. Each new kid, they buy a ring. So everyone can see, three rings – this bloke's fathered three kids.'

Was this true, or some boozy wind-up? As the boys pointed out, it's hard to imagine anyone further removed from a babyfather than me. Still, I quite liked the idea of a ring. It was preferable to the slap in the face or rather knee in the balls of the male ego represented by some of the, uh, more 'permanent tokens' that can come your way on becoming a dad – 'New Dad' mugs, pinnies bearing the legend 'Say It Loud, I'm a Dad and I'm Proud!', Y-fronts announcing 'Look Out! New Dad Coming Through!' I liked it more than another of the evening's proposals: that I get a tattoo – a little day/month/year tag which seemed to me as if it might wind up looking and feeling like my own personal sell-by date. In fact, I'm still thinking about a ring. I might just get around to it one day.

I couldn't prevaricate about the christening, however. I had to get on with it. I didn't exactly go quietly though. I had my qualms. I began to wonder whether Kim and I hadn't already celebrated Lee's birth. Admittedly we'd done it a long time before she actually appeared, but wasn't that appropriate to our technologically accelerated times. The occasion in question was Kim's first ultrasound scan, around four months into the pregnancy. Obviously this is an important and potentially problematic part of ante-natal care. But if everything's all right, if you discover that your child is growing without any great complications, the whole thing takes on a kind of celebratory air, a more than medical significance.

There were several middle-class couples in the waiting room when we went to St Tommy's for our scan. It made me wonder whether the whole thing wasn't almost the 'couples' era' equivalent of a christening: a virtual birth and techno-baptism rolled into one, with a natty point and click interface substituting for the font. Much like the real-world version, you can, if you've planned ahead and want to know the sex of your child, come out with the name sorted and a photograph to remember it all by. Given our blind faith in technology and the fact that we don't have to put up with the physical consequences of having something grow inside us, men can come out of the whole thing with the impression that it's all over bar the shouting. Virtually speaking, they're already dads. They have the pictures to prove it.

For our scan, we planned to take the afternoon off, wander down the South Bank afterwards, watch the Thames, generally try to take in what was happening to us, aided by a small black and white profile shot of our future child. In the end we were stymied by the fact that Lee wasn't in quite the right position to wink at the camera. In fact, Kim would have to go back for another scan in order to complete the full medical check. By that time, I would be out of the country working. But even so, we still spent an afternoon idling significantly by the river.

But the problem with the scan as surrogate christening, I now concluded, was that the only people involved were Kim and me. I didn't like the idea that parenting was just about that modern social unit – the couple. I wanted to get friends and family involved in some way. I thought about designing my own non-religious alternative christening. Some friends had come up with a wedding ceremony of their own. Staunch republicans and atheists, they didn't want the Church or the State involved in their union. So they dreamed up this ceremony which involved things like hopping over broomsticks in various charged locations in the East End of London. Then for some reason they dropped the idea at the last minute, went the more conventional route – register office then pub crawl afterwards.

I'm not sure why they pulled out. I guess they had their reasons. But I admired the idea and the effort they put in. It was, I had to admit, beyond me. When it comes to DIY, I can barely get it together to put up a set of shelves. Knocking up a whole alternative christening ceremony was, I decided, way out of my league. Briefly I turned to the idea of a pagan ceremony. Superficially, paganism sounds quite attractive – all that stuff about it being the true religion of these ancient isles, suppressed by conquering Christians, altogether more in touch with the planet. But, once you start to seriously consider it – messing about with mystically significant flowers and twigs, hanging out with people who call themselves druids – it begins to seem like the kind of thing Edina from *Ab Fab* might contemplate.

It looked as though the Church was pretty much the only game in town. I constructed little for and against lists about it all in my head. For: it would be an excuse for a party; the family would like it; I liked the idea of godparents – not so much the spiritual guidance side of the deal but the thought that you could involve your friends, put together a sort of alternative extended family, plus, on a purely acquisitive level, it meant Lee would get extra presents for birthday and Christmas. Against: I was being a total hypocrite. The problem with this kind of thing, however, is that no one ever tells you how you actually add up the final balance. I talked it over with Kim. She didn't believe either, but pointed out that that wasn't necessarily an obstacle as far as the Church of England was concerned. She'd spent part of her childhood in a smallish village and had sung in the local church choir. Even then, she said, it seemed to be less about God and more about family life. So perhaps I should stop thinking about the christening as the return of my Catholic past.

She had a point, though, sad to say, the ultimate decider as far as my deliberations were concerned was standard-issue masculine laziness. Actually objecting to a religious ceremony, holding to my socalled principles, would require some effort. And my energy levels – never very high – were starting to dip. The regular 2 a.m. wake ups and dawn starts were beginning to bite. With the christening, I really didn't have to do an awful lot. Kim's sister had already sorted out the church (an atmospheric ancient pile somewhere near Portishead, a nowhere suburb of Bristol, best known as the home town of the appropriately melancholy eponymous band). She was handling the invites. The party afterwards would be at their house. All I had to do was supply addresses for guests from my side of the family and offer an opinion on what sandwiches we should have for tea afterwards.

So in the end I sort of reconciled myself to it. Just shut up and enjoy it, I told myself. But I was making a big assumption here, that once I was fine with the Church, it would be fine with me. We could send out the invites, start filling up the font. I didn't stop to think that the Church might have to reconcile itself to someone like me. I figured they'd be happy to chalk another one up for Jesus, no questions asked. A big mistake.

Word came, a couple of months before the February ceremony, that the vicar wanted to see us – there were forms he had to sign before the christening could go ahead. He also seemed a bit worried about the state of our relationship. Kim's sister had told him that we weren't married and he seemed to have come away with the idea that we were the inner-city couple of tabloid stereotype, that I was indeed some kind of south London babyfather, cruising round town, fingers clanking with semi-precious symbols of my feckless virility, while Kim was the lone, single mum, abandoned, destitute, struggling to bring up a child on her own.

Kim went down to see him (conveniently, I was away working again) and pointed out that while we might not be married, we had actually been together for about twelve years. However, he did pick up on her general ambivalence about the whole subject. (While I thought marriage was not such a great idea, Kim wasn't quite so sure. We'd talked about it on and off over the years – and were about to talk about it a whole lot more, thanks to the vicar.) Why didn't we get married? he suggested. We were obviously committed to each other. He could make a few calls, shift a few things around, see if he couldn't do us a nice Christmas wedding. All we had to do was say the word.

When Kim came back from the meeting, she told me that the vicar wanted to see me before signing the form. He wants to know why we're not married, she said pointedly. I think I muttered something about how even the C of E was going in for performance-related pay these days, that even vicars had quotas to fill and targets to meet. But I was pretty worried. I had hoped it would all be sorted out after he'd met Kim and I could just nip in and out quickly on the day. This wasn't only laziness on my part. I still had enough neurotic energy to worry that, by going ahead with the christening, I was acting in bad faith. I felt like I was being rather underhand.

The thing was, for all my qualms, by now I certainly didn't want the christening not to happen. Too much was riding on it. Everyone thought a double christening was a wonderful idea. I'd even been roped in as godfather to Lee's cousin. (I dutifully pointed out that I was a godless infidel and, hence, not perhaps the best choice to watch over Lydia's future spiritual health. She didn't seem to mind.) So I went down to see the vicar, one Monday morning in January, three weeks or so before the main event. He wasn't what I expected; not like the Catholic priests of my youth, more like a cheerfully brusque schoolteacher. Perhaps that's why, at first, I felt uncomfortably like some sort of naughty schoolboy.

As things went on, I began to see myself as somehow similar to a government minister being grilled on *Newsnight* by Paxman. Not that he adopted a hard-core interrogation technique. It's more that, when Paxman starts in on Michael Howard, or whoever, he's generally got reason, logic and common sense on his side. He's already won the argument. So the only thing Howard can do is ignore the questions, keep talking until time runs out and hope his press people can spin the whole thing as a defiant performance. Terrible though it is to admit, for the duration of my morning tea with the vicar, I was Michael Howard. He had logic and common sense on his side. I could see his point. I really could. But I resolved to keep talking and hope that eventually he would get tired and give in.

We started on marriage. Once he had glanced at my ringless fingers and established that, as Kim suggested, I wasn't exactly a candidate in the Babyfather of the Year play-offs, he tried a different tack. By not marrying Kim, I was responsible, indirectly, for legions of single mothers struggling on their own, for the moral and economic decline of family life in the inner cities. I might not have been flitting irresponsibly from bedroom to bedroom, but I was doing my bit. I was a babyfather by proxy, as it were. So I should marry Kim to make a statement to the people around me. At the time, we lived on Landor Road, one of the main drug-dealing strips in south London. I was fairly sure that most of the people I passed in the street had more pressing things on their mind than checking up on the latest in the local paper's births, deaths and marriages column.

But I thought it best not to mention that and instead shifted the discussion on to politics and economics. Not such a bad move, as it turned out. He happily took up the bait, pondered the CSA, the Welfare State, the awfulness of the Tory Party, the problems with the Labour Party ('The trouble with socialists is that they don't understand original sin'). All this gave me some breathing space, but eventually he came back and landed his killer blow. If, for various reasons, I couldn't see the point in getting married, why did I want to christen my child? 'A good excuse for a knees up' clearly wasn't the answer he was looking for. I muttered something or other about passing on Christian values and somehow, luckily, we got back on to politics again. As we went on (we talked for over an hour) I kept saying to myself, don't say it, don't mention that you don't believe in God. Visions of Basil Fawlty yelling, 'Don't mention the war!' danced before my eyes.

In the end he got tired of me, I think. He smiled, said it had been enjoyable talking to me and that he'd see me at the christening. I was home free. But before I went, I thought I'd just clear something up. One of the godparents we'd picked, an old friend of mine, was Jewish. Was that OK? He gave me a 'You really are taking the piss now, my son' look. 'I'm afraid I can't have that,' he said. I briefly considered saying that it shouldn't be that much of an issue, because, though nominally Jewish, Graham was like me, he didn't actually believe in God either. But instead I told him I'd ask my brother to substitute.

Christenings are, by nature, rather subdued affairs. They're not like weddings. With all those tipsy bridesmaids, boozy best men and speeches packed with dirty jokes, stuff can happen at weddings. But by the time you get to christenings, stuff has already happened and you're living with the consequences. Ours was a pretty quiet affair, though I can't remember that much about it. Lee had begun to come down with a mild case of childhood eczema. It was nothing serious, but she scratched herself awake most nights. I felt like I'd only just started to discover what tiredness was – whole new vistas of complete and total exhaustion seemed to be opening up in front of me.

I do remember that it was cold and grey, a typical February day. I remember Graham, my rejected kosher godfather, and his girlfriend got lost on the way down to Portishead but made it in the end. I remember that Lee puked on my shoulder as we went in to the church. She was wearing a sort of black velvet party dress from Gap. It would be different, we thought. Now it looked as if it had been deliberately chosen to highlight regurgitated milk and the various skin creams Lee had been prescribed.

I don't remember hearing any of the stuff about 'renouncing Satan' that seemed to be a part of the Catholic christenings I had attended as a child. In fact the whole thing was pleasantly informal. At times it seemed close to some kind of media event. At the start the vicar came on a bit like the warm-up man for a TV gameshow. 'I understand we have some people here who've come all the way from Peckham ... is that right?' I'm not sure what the people from Peckham (Nicky and Russell, Lee's other godparents) were supposed to do in reponse. Probably not give him the woof, I guess. At the end, he hoiked Lee up in the air and wandered around showing her to the congregation. It reminded me of something similar in *The Lion King*. Incredibly, Lee didn't cry. Afterwards, the church was lit up by a barrage of flash guns as various sets of parents (one other baby was being christened as well) got their pictures by the font. Sorting out everyone's photographs seemed to take as much time as the ceremony itself.

Looking at them now, they're a bit like pictures from the wedding we never had. There are lots of group shots outside the church, various family members clustered round Lee, Kim (looking tired but beautiful) and me (looking completely wrecked). There are a fair few font ensembles, all featuring the vicar sporting a huge toothy smile. These have been the source of some sniggering among friends. It's been suggested more than once that he did indeed look like an ecclesiastical gameshow host. I understand what they mean, but my theory is that he was just trying to make sure he didn't ruin anybody's pictures. With people flashing away from all sides, I think he figured that his best bet was to adopt a pleasant fixed grin. Behind the superficially cheesy smile I can see a kind of charity. And I remember that I never really thanked him on the day and that I should have done, if for nothing else than for letting me get away with it all.

A while ago, I read a column in an American men's mag, written by a dad-to-be, who had only just managed to conceive but had already rushed into print to ponder the effects of fatherhood on his life. It had come at just the right time, he figured. The pleasures of his twentynothing youth – the party-hearty decadence, the existential freedom, the bungee jumping – were all beginning to pall. It was time to sort himself out. As his child edged towards consciousness, he too could finally get a life. Even as his baby grew, he too could feel himself growing up.

Americans can turn pretty much anything into an opportunity for 'personal growth', but I find it hard to be too snide about this. I think I was a victim of the same delusion, kidded myself I would instantly attain maturity, achieve a sort of gravitas-to-go. Perhaps it's a function of what you might call womb envy. As their girlfriends or wives begin to visibly expand, men feel the need for some kind of development too. So they experience a sort of phantom pregnancy of the mind. Somewhere deep inside, they start to nurture a secret, half-formed fantasy about scales dropping from eyes and finally seeing things clearly.

This is a pretty dumb idea but it's easily cured. A few days of actually being a dad usually does the trick. In the first weeks after Lee was born, I managed to achieve all the maturity and gravitas of an E-head who's necked a handful of doves on an empty stomach. Afterwards, as exhaustion replaced elation, I could pretty much feel myself getting more and more stupid by the minute; I could feel my synapses fizzling out one by one, to be replaced by something with all the mental agility of cotton wool. Far from becoming clearer, life actually became very unclear. The world became a much more complex and confusing place. I wasn't quite sure how to go about things, how I felt, what I believed.

Anyway, that's my excuse for the tangle I got into over the christening. I am pleased we did it, pleased especially that Kim's grandmother was able to enjoy the day so much. She died a few months later. I'm happy that we did something to celebrate Lee's birth, something that wasn't just some jokey male rite of passage, something that was about more than me and Kim, something that brought in the wider world. I just wish I could have achieved all this without inviting God to the party. It turned out that I could have, fairly easily. Shortly after our day in church, someone told me about humanist christening ceremonies. So I'll know what to do next time, if there is a next time; but in a way, I wish I hadn't found this out. It just heightened my sense that, good as the ceremony was, it wasn't quite there. I didn't get things quite right, didn't quite hit the mark. I was close – but no cigar. Still, perhaps it was, after all, the perfect preparation for fatherhood. I suspect I'm going to have to get used to feeling that way quite a bit over the next few years.

John Hegley

John Hegley was born in Newington Green, where he is now living with a small family of his own. He recently had his own series on Radio 4 (*Hearing with Hegley*), has a collection of poems out (*The Family Pack*) and is currently broadening his performance repertoire into the movement area. For many years he had long periods of undisturbed sleep.

There's Not a Lot of Kip When There's a Nipper in the Night

John Hegley pens an ode to sleep

When we were two
sleep was cheap.
When we had no one to keep
us from sleep
a heap of sleep was easily come by.
The good old nights.
The well-rested phase.
When we were two
we really didn't realize sleep's value.
But when there were three of us
we knew.

Sleep.
The seldom stuff.
How difficult to creep across the floor quietly enough.
The soreness and the ache
of being narrowly awake.
The dreaming of a break.
Without the dreaming,
the bleariness
and blinking,
the little low peep
signalling another bout of early-morning drinking.
The tiny life.
The big deprivation.
The mother and father are in further
education.

James Hawes

James Hawes is one of five children. He had an idyllic childhood in Edinburgh, followed by a hideous adolescence in Shropshire; then a great time at college, followed by five years in go-hang-yourself bedsits. He is currently on sabbatical from lecturing in the German department at University College, Swansea. His first novel, A *White Merc With Fins*, was published in 1996 by Jonathan Cape, two weeks after the birth of his first child, Owain. Cape brought out his second novel, *Rancid Aluminium*, in May 1997, and will publish his third later (God willing): he hopes to have more kids to go with the books.

Why Not to Dash Your Baby's Brains Out

James Hawes stages a
cathartic rant

The other night I stopped dead and realized with terror that my
neighbours must have been able to hear every word I was saying, let
alone groaning or shouting. The poor sods must have been halfway
to calling the cops or the social services.

I mean, if you *didn't* call social services when you heard what *they*
had just heard, you would lie awake wondering if tomorrow you
would read in the papers: HEARTLESS BRITAIN #46: NEIGHBOURS
HOGSNORE WHILE INNOCENT BABY HAS BRAINS DASHED OUT.
Because what they must just have been hearing through the wall was
a raving dialogue between one adult male voice and a wailing baby.

I can give you the words, but you will have to supply the wailing
sound-track for yourself. If you have been there, it will be no problem. You will know the ear-tearing horror of a baby's wails, which
have been genetically designed, in far harder times, in order to cause
maximum possible stress. Whatever you are in the middle of, it is
purpose-created to blow every fuse you have. You could be putting
the finishing touches to a cave-painting masterpiece, or telling Ug
and the lads about the last sabre-tooth you almost killed, or you
could be just about getting beyond first-base flea-grooming with the
Uma Thurman of the Cro-Magnon world, and be eyeing the

landscape for a handy thicket of bushes ... and then baby lets loose.

There is no such thing as flexible response here. Pamper-arse will make the same fucking horrible racket whether he has just woken up for no reason or had a ten-storey building collapse around him. His reaction will be the same: *stop the world!* And he has just the weapon to do it: that terrible, mind-searing wailing. Like I said: if you know it, you know.

And don't gloat if you don't: because, despite thousands of years of education and rational advance, the odds are still heavily on that *you will.* Think of *that* as you blithely swill designer lager on Clapham Common, without a care in the world, bastard features.

[Director's note: the WAILING BABY remains entirely monotonous throughout; the ADULT MALE VOICE starts ironically, but gradually becomes wilder and more alarming. Irony cannot cope with this weight of reality.]

ADULT MALE: OK, OK, Baby, now that's enough, isn't it? You're not hungry or wet or cold or alone, and there are no sabre-toothed tigers in this time-zone. See?

BABY: Wail!

ADULT MALE: All right then, let's sing your favourite song, shall we? Yes, there there: *Will ye no' come back again, will ye no' come back again* ... Oh shit. Yes, well, I'm sorry, but it's your mother who should be doing this. Oh, shut up, will you! Now look here, Baby, if you don't stop crying you'll *go to Public School*, understand? And you know what will happen to you in the dorms. Well, no, I hope you don't just yet. But I mean it. I do.

BABY: Wail!

ADULT MALE: I see. Right. Oh, God. Darling! Daaarling! Ah, I see your mother's got her earplugs in again. All right for some. OH, GOD, I must have been insane! Stop it for ... OK, sorry, Baby. Sorry. Daddy's sorry. Nice and quiet now. Listen: the Baby Whisperer cures all, the Baby Whisperer says: *Go to sleep, go to sleeeep* ...

BABY: Wail!

ADULT MALE: Look, I think we need to be straight about this, Baby: Daddy was genetically designed to shag around and wander about doing the odd bit of hunting now and then, OK? Well, I'm all for compromise, but I have my demands too, you know. I do. Yes, I do. Like sleep. Remember that? Oh, Christ. Now, you know what's going to happen to you if you don't shut up, don't you? Daddy's going to buy a Volvo with extra seats in the back and he's going to *put you in the crumple zone!* Yes, he is. Oh, fuck fuck fuck fuck fuck. There's nothing bloody wrong with you, you little ...

BABY: Wail!

ADULT MALE: You're not mine. That's it. You're not, are you? Keep crying if you're not my son. There, I knew it. Ha! Right, we are definitely going to have a DNA test done on you before you get a penny of my hard-earned. Oh, Jesus. Please please please stop, dear Baby. I can't stand it any more. Stop! That's enough! Please!! I see, it's like that, is it? A battle to the death between your DNA and mine, huh? Well bad luck, Pantload, I'm bigger than you, and my social persona is wearing thin. Just think of me as a silverback. Oh, give me fucking strength! *Mony's the hert would brak in twa, should ye no' come back again* (all together now), *Will ye no' come ...*

BABY: Wail!

ADULT MALE: So, a battle of wills, is it? Fair enough. You asked for it. *So you see, Lootenant, they say Keyser Soze had this little baby son back in Turkey; his pride and joy, they say. But then this baby tried to match his will-power with Keyser Soze. So Keyser Soze showed his baby what will-power REALLY was ...*

BABY: Wail!

ADULT MALE: Sorry. Sorry. I only *thought* about it. I was only joking. OH GODDDDD! Right. *Finito. Basta. Schweinhund* Baby, for you the crying is over! If you don't stop in three seconds it's you or me, Baby: three seconds, then I'm going to have to dash your brains out, got it? One ... two ... Ahhhh! *Wiillll ye no' come back again ...*

[Director's note: This dialogue is played in a continuous loop for three hours or until the audience starts committing acts of violence.]

I mean. What if I had slipped with him right then? How, with the neighbours' evidence, could I have convinced social services that I had not dashed his brains out deliberately?

Well, here's the defence: it is not my fault. I refuse to accept any blame for this behaviour. And this is not because I am genetically less designed to wipe arse at 3 a.m. than my wife. The idea of the Selfish Gene is interesting and defensible, but the notion of a Sexist Chromosome is plain crap. If that were true, how come the world is full of women happily putting off sprogging until as late as possible? If it was all about Men and Women, then the world would be full of men running a mile from kids and women screaming to have them. Which it ain't. Maybe the Biological Clock ticks differently; maybe men don't hear Rutger Hauer saying *time to breed* until about five years later than women. But we all hear the same voice when it comes. Every prosperous part of the world is inhabited largely by Men 'n' Women who are both of the opinion that rug-rats are an important thing to do, but are best done late and few. Even in Ireland (where six or seven sibs is nothing uncommon among my thirtysomething friends) the birth-rate has gone through the floor in the last few years. No, it is not my fault and it is not my sexist chromosomes.

It is the fault of two things which are the curse and glory of Western Civilization: our obsession with Equality and our half-baked concept of Free Will.

The Equality problem is this: if we are (as we all believe these days) equally important in the world, with equal rights and suchlike, well then: why on earth should I allow this baby to trample all over my life?

Sure, Baby has his rights too – but since when did anyone have the right to indulge themselves by ruining someone else's life? And, if we are all equal, if no one is allowed to have moral privileges of birth or need, why the hell should a *baby* be so special? Just because it's the future of the human race? So what? Why should the future of the human race be any more special than the *present*? I mean, Oprah, don't we present-dwellers have *a right to our lives* as well?

Then add half-baked ideas of Free Will. We can see the results of this best if we look at Yankland, because we are all becoming Yanks rapidly in this sense. Or rather: the Yanks are already what we are going to become, as usual. *No one is prepared to accept that anything is just bad luck.* Everything that goes wrong in our lives has to be someone's *fault*; someone's *free will.* And if you chose, freely, to have a baby, then when you naturally discover that it has ruined your life, you can only blame two people: yourself, or the baby. But here's where the half-baked bit comes in, fatally: no one blames *themselves* for anything in America. Which leaves baby holding the bottle.

The time cannot be far off when some New Rich White Trash Yank couple will sue their own baby for Gross Lifestyle Infringement or whatever. Or sue the gynaecologist for not having a Pursuit of Happiness warning on his desk, saying *The State of California is aware that having babies can totally fuck you up.*

Being European, I am still just about capable of blaming myself for things. Which makes the only logical conclusion, at 3 a.m.: *I must have been off my fucking head!!*

You stand there, knackered from months of nights like this already, doing a task which any undisturbed ten-year-old or any unsenile 85-year-old could do. I mean, where is the logic in that?

No, what we need are proper State-run baby-overnight hotels.

In these wonderful, beneficent institutions, brainless and unqualified teenagers would do their GCSEs in Infant Care Studies, as vocational preparation for the teenage parenthood certainly awaiting them. They would also get an allowance, funded joyously by the parents of the babies. And they would be held under permanent, strict and Draconian supervision by retired ward sisters.

In this way, the young and old of society would have a vital role to play, i.e. child-minding, the same role they play in every non-industrialized society. This would stop them getting into glue-sniffing or gin, vandalism or despair, respectively.

And meanwhile the thirtysomethings, who have invested vast amounts of their own and society's time and money in getting qualified and trained, could get on with earning the money to pay the tax that keeps the whole sodding ship afloat.

And going out for drinks again. And going out for meals again. And going on hols again. Oh, God. Never again. And to think there were times when I chose *voluntarily* not to go out in the evening!

And don't you dare start going on with all that crap about 'but it's so rewarding to see baby smile', and 'but he does love you really, see how he recognizes you'. Yes, it is nice and yes, it works. But let us be straight as to why.

Baby smiles at adults – at any old adult – because Baby is

evolutionarily designed to smile, just in case said adult is thinking about dashing his brains out. Like lion cubs, who roll over, as if to be tickled, in a vain attempt to stop the New Boss Lion killing them so that his genes make it into the next generation. Darling Baby smiling is just Darling Baby doing the only defence-mechanism he has got. It is *not* because he lurves you. He is just tapping into your programmed responses.

Love? Come on. Look: my baby has wrecked my wife's and my life, work and health for the last six months (thereby, incidentally, probably damaging his own chances in the long run). Whether by sheer coincidence or deep evolutionary cunning ('No siblings, please, all for *me*!') this has had the result of devastating our sex life as well. He has, in short, utterly fucked us over. And here's the great bit: if, after all these nights and weeks of hell, if, after all this lunatic dedication of two entire adult lives to one baby, we two were killed by a runaway steamroller tomorrow, and he survived, what would he remember of us? Zilcho. Nix. Bugger-all. He would smile delightfully at the first Adoption Agency clients that looked at him. And *they*, of course, would believe it too.

I am not some heartless bastard. I am just trying to correct all this horrible schmaltzy, sentimental crap about babies. Babies are not people, they are problems to be coped with until they start becoming people. God, if I ever get another invite to some friends' baby's first birthday party 'signed' by the loving parents *and the baby*, I swear I shall go round and Kalashnikov the lot of them for offences against truthfulness and human dignity.

So now I will get accused of not loving Baby enough. Well, I consider it rationally impossible to love and adore someone who wakes you up four times a night for no apparent reason. You could be shacked up with Uma Thurman, but if it turned out that she was a loony who woke you up four times every night just to moan and whinge about nothing much, you simply would not stick it.

Babies should only be born at the age of one. And since that isn't evolutionarily possible, they should be kept in nice, bright, warm, stimulating State-run baby hotels till they are one.

At least one. You think that would stymie your baby's intellectual development? Think again: your baby *has* no intellectual development. It has a genetic potential, yes, but that is given and undisturbable (that's the whole point of genetic potential). Meanwhile its socialization (the other half of its nature-to-be) has not kicked in. All Baby wants – since all babies are by nature C2s – is to have warm, stuffy rooms, brightly coloured wallpaper (preferably fluffy), lots of jingly-jangly noises, plenty of physical contact and inane chit-chat. *And he doesn't give a toss who provides it.*

Sure, I admit things get different once they can walk and talk and stick their hands in electric sockets and stuff. I intend to cope with this change. I intend to say: *Ah, yes, Baby, now I'm your father, d'you see? You haven't seen much of me for a while, but I hear you're sort of walking and talking and suchlike now. Splendid. Splendid. Right, well, I must be off now. Um, look here: you'll be going away to school in a little while, and then, well, we'll have a chat when you're about twenty-one eh? Thank you, Nanny.*

And don't tell me it gets better. I know it does. Yes, I am looking forward to seeing him in his Paddy Clarke years, that brief little idyll when you can read and ride your bike but are untroubled by sexual adrenalin. Yes, that will be great. *But then he will become a teenager!* Ugh! He will lie about, smelling out the house and squeezing spots and sulking because I can't afford to buy him the vintage eighties VW GTi Cabrio which (like teenagers of all ages), he is convinced will deliver the fabled sex life he just *knows* exists somewhere. And generally hating me because I am an old toss who, as far as he can see, hasn't Got A Life. And he will probably be right, because I will probably have wasted it looking after him and his sibs.

I now realize why my friends who went to boarding schools seem to get on better with their parents than normal people do: by getting shot of the brats sharpish, Mummy and Daddy have had the time to keep up their own lives.

But.

But there *are* good things about having a baby. Four, to be exact.

One: you get thin because you can never go to the pub again. Among my thirtysomething pals, the average automatic post-natal weight loss seems to be about ten pounds over the first six months.

Two: you can lust openly at attractive women as you walk about with your baby-carrier on your shoulders. They smile back. It is a well-known fact that a single man+baby is the world's easiest model to shift. Again, this is nothing to do with women's biology, it is all to do with social signs: the fact that you are dragging Shite-Drawers about with you means that you are not some self-obsessed, own-pectoral-worshipping navel-gazer who is incapable of considering anyone's life to be as important as his own. Which, given the number of men who very clearly fit this category, is understandably attractive to women.

Three: when you get up from the floor, holding your baby in one arm, you get this really weird flashback to being an ape. Great fun.

Four: as you wheel your pram around endlessly at 3 a.m. you learn that Equality is bollocks, and you see the real meaning of Free Will.

Equality is gone, because you know that if some party of psycho-skins came round the corner, you would, without question or hesitation, put your head in front of a machete aimed at your baby. I didn't say it was logical, I said it happens.

And as for Free Will, you will realize that all that ranting is just you being a baby too; just you crying out to some mythical mother, or mother-state, to come and help you. And now you know they are not coming. You have chosen, it was your own decision, and now you have to live with it. For how long? you ask. And the Court of Free Will replies (as it always does): *for as long as it takes*.

At this point you realize the strange, uncanny paradox of Free Will, which is this: it alters the world. The world in which we make our free decisions is not the world in which we have to live with them. The moment you decided to have this baby, of your own free will, you ended your freedom to choose. You chose duty, which is the opposite of freedom.

Or maybe the beginning of a different freedom. Because now the real miracle happens: *time stops counting*. As you wheel your pram about, or bounce your baby for hours in a darkened room, you are doing absolutely nothing. And yet time passes incredibly quickly. Or rather: it passes quickly *because* you are doing nothing – nothing, that is, by the standards of goal-obsessed, stressed-out, control-freak workaholics.

You have finally been forced to get off the mouse-wheel. You have been driven, without intending it, into the position of mental and physical exhaustion which is the standard precursor of meditation. Which is why I advise you not to dash your baby's brains out. Yes, your baby is stopping you doing all sorts of things you used to do. But maybe, somehow, that is the whole point. Maybe it is actually what you wanted.

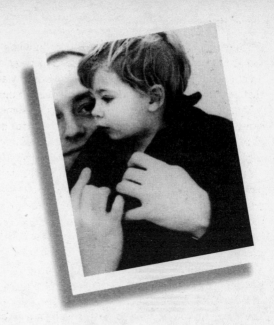

Peter Howarth

Peter Howarth lives in south
London with his partner,
Tracey, and their son Jackson.
He is currently the editor
of *Esquire* magazine. He
has worked in the fashion
business and for *GQ* and *Arena*
magazines, and has written for
the likes of the *Guardian* and
L'Uomo Vogue. He is happy to
have been asked to edit this
anthology, and happier still that
Jackson's arrival qualified
him for the job.

Second Childhood

Peter Howarth discovers
male bonding

There are no photographs of my father and me as a child. No tired, pale patriarch proudly cradling a swaddled bundle in the anaemic glow of NHS neon; no doting chauffeur steering precious buggy-cargo round the bleak winter monochrome of the local park; no first birthday magician bearing brightly coloured balloons and wrapping paper to his captivated audience; no seaside architect, faithful brickie in sun-hat by his side, constructing a brave new world out of sodden, dull Margate sand; no England manager coaching his barely mobile star centre-forward – white T-shirt, blue shorts – in the back garden. No photographs.

My father was a photographer in the sixties, and up until the age of fourteen, I only really knew him through a set of pictures taken at my parents' wedding by a friend of his, another professional. Here were the happy couple, snapped Magnum-style in period black and white. Caught moments from the big day: my mother, impossibly young, blond and beautiful, lifting the veil over her head; my father, also young, dark, Roman profile, a glass suspended in his hand as he imperiously surveyed the reception.

The pictures put a face to a name, and helped explain how I had got here. The story, as told to me by my mother, was this: she had met my father in Swinging London, a young Austrian girl who'd run away from home; he had swept her off her feet, a glamorous Cambridge graduate who hung out with Peter Cook and the Establishment crowd, and had proposed to her in an underground station after a whirlwind six-week romance. She had accepted, and they were married in style in a small church by his mother's stately house in Cumbria (the setting of those pictures).

They had adventures, did my mum and dad. He asked her, with eyes closed, to put a pin in an atlas to choose their honeymoon desti-nation. Weeks later, she found herself Africa-bound. He took pictures for the Sunday supplements; they went to sixties parties; they had groovy brunches in their flat in Kensington, where the bright young things of the day would drop round and swap gossip. Africa became an obsession. They returned to cover the East African Safari. At one point, Dad had to come back to England to deliver some film. My mother stayed in a mission and waited. When he reappeared he sheepishly confessed to having had a one-night stand at a party in London. She forgave him. Then it transpired that the other woman was pregnant. She could not forgive him. They split up. She was expecting too at the time – me – but did not know it. I was diagnosed as a phantom pregnancy – indigestion. But, inevitably, I became a reality and was born to a single parent on 12 September 1964 at St Mary Abbot's Hospital, Kensington. My father sent red roses. My mother ripped them to pieces.

This was the legacy my father left me: a tale of romance, glamour and, ultimately, disappointment. My mother never denied his exis-tence, but he could only really exist for me in my imagination. As the years passed, I assembled a more fleshed-out portrait – always through my mother's stories – and the man I created for myself became a defining character in my childish life.

You see, as expressed by my mother, my father was a kind of tragic hero. An engineering graduate who could fix cars with his bare hands; a philanthropist who gave away a gun to a black South African priest to aid the struggle against apartheid; a star photographer, published in *Life*, who made a name for himself by being able to get *the* picture, whatever the difficulty or the danger; a talent so versatile that he later became an award-winning documentary film maker. This was the man who had sired me. Nothing to be ashamed of in those genes.

But, as with all tragic heroes, as well as his undoubted gifts, he also possessed a flaw: a feckless irresponsibility. This manifested itself most clearly in his inability to handle money, to keep promises and to sustain a faithful relationship. I could never forget (or forgive) the fact that this man had left my mother and me to fend for ourselves, while he pursued his high-minded trajectory.

And so the true legacy my father bequeathed me was a contradictory desire: to both be like him, and to be nothing like him whatsoever. If I'm honest about it, I have to admit that these twin feelings have, until recently, been the driving forces of my life. As a child, teenager and young adult, I desperately wanted to emulate my old man. I too would be a romantic creative (I painted, I played in bands, I read poetry), I too would be part of the *demi-monde* (I bought the clothes, dyed my hair, went to the parties), I too would be an academic achiever (like him I went to Cambridge). At the same time, I would make amends for his flakiness. There was to be no flaw in the hero I would strive to become – I would start by being my mother's right-hand man, a grown-up and sensible son; in time I would prove myself a studious student and successful employee.

So strong and established were these convictions and the corresponding picture I had created of my father, that when I finally met him, on my fourteenth birthday, the reality could do nothing to displace the myth. He didn't have to do or say much to confirm my preconceptions. He seemed suitably enigmatic – older and more grizzled than in the well-thumbed wedding photos, and now sporting a full beard. But I thought I had his number. God knows what he thought of his barely teenage son, already so convinced he was a match for the adult world.

You see, and I'll venture a dangerous generalization here, the sons of absent fathers have to grow up fast. In my case I had to become the missing man in my mother's life – I had to be the male about the house. But the problem was, I had no reliable role model. Sure, my mother did have a few boyfriends, some of whom were with her for years at a time; but, try as I might to adopt them, there was always the sense that I was in competition with these men, rather than the object of their freely given love and affection. And so my relationship with my imaginary father was strengthened, not weakened, by the appearance of these interlopers. This was a thing between me and him. If I did have any surrogate father figures, they were to be found away from home – teachers at school, friends' dads, tutors at university and eventually employers.

I grew up fast all right. I could hold my own in adult conversation by the time I turned nine, I travelled to secondary school on the bus and tube by myself aged ten, I worked in the summer holidays from fourteen, lost my virginity at fifteen and at sixteen had embarked on a three-year relationship with a divorcée six years my senior. I passed my driving test at seventeen, held down a full-time job between school and university at eighteen, and on graduating, at twenty-one, took up a position as a projects manager for a high-profile fashion designer.

But though I thought I was equal to this accelerated development, I paid a price. I was without doubt given to an over-serious disposition. Because I had persuaded myself that I was not so much following in my father's footsteps as trying to wear his shoes, I had a sense that life was a very serious business indeed. Not surprisingly, my ease with adults was mirrored by a corresponding unease with children my own age; the friendships I struck up tended to be with older kids, or those as precociously earnest as myself. In particular, I found it hard to develop strong and lasting male friendships. I was fine with women; I'd grown up in a female-dominated household and felt I knew pretty much what made them tick. But while this proved invaluable in my efforts to be a tousle-haired song-writing romantic, it made me develop a mistrust of my own sex. Men were the foreign territory, women the familiar homestead.

When I became a freelance journalist in my mid-twenties, I wrote a piece for *Arena* magazine about male bonding. In it I proposed the view that men don't really like each other in the way that women do – that instead of an all-embracing sense of solidarity with their brothers, men clash antlers in some primal way, trying to outdo each other, trying to put one over on each other. I cited the example of a stag night I had recently attended, where the groom was playfully tortured by being kept awake all night, despite his clear desire to rest his alcohol-befuddled head. Each time he'd fall asleep on his bed, his 'friends' would burst into the room, guitars and percussive bottles and cutlery at the ready, to blast him awake with a rendition of 'Viva España'. By contrast, I pointed out that the bride-to-be had gone off for a civilized weekend in the country with her nearest and dearest female friends, where wine and good conversation were the order of the evening. I concluded that this was proof positive of the male of the species being socially less well adjusted than his mate.

Someone wrote to the magazine suggesting that I clearly didn't have any good male friends, or any notion of what male friendship was. I realize now he was probably right, though at the time I dismissed the idea as facetious. But slowly, through the years, it became apparent that my hardened mistrust of my fellow man was clearly tempered by a sentimental yearning for something I was missing. I'd find myself gripped by the most cack-handed, third-rate, late-night-TV buddy movie. And as for tales of fathers and sons – well, I knew something was up when I found myself bawling at a scene in *Sleepless in Seattle*; not where hero and heroine finally clinch in the inevitable, overblown denouement, but earlier, in a small quiet scene where Tom Hanks is playing American football with his son on the beach. Gulp. The girl I was with at the time thought this was pathetic coming from a grown man and didn't think anything of telling me so.

But what she didn't realize (and what I would have vehemently denied at the time) was that I wasn't a grown man. For all my bravado and apparent maturity, I was in fact still the fatherless child of some twenty-odd years ago. How could I really be anything else? I didn't know how to be anything else. There had been no one to teach me.

A year or so on, everything changed. The girl in *Sleepless in Seattle* – not Meg Ryan but Tracey, the one who'd sat next to me and taken the piss so loudly after my waterworks – got pregnant. And for the first time in my life, I was not going to be a phoney grown-up: I was going to be the real thing.

My son Jackson was born on 3 July 1995 at St Thomas's Hospital. Unlike my father before me, I was at his birth. I had been ministering the gas and air through the night, trying to be of use; things had gone slowly at first, and then frighteningly fast. Tracey's waters broke, she needed an epidural, the child wouldn't come out, and I watched, worried sick, as its heart beat decreased on the foetal monitor every time she pushed. Finally, I was reduced to the role of horrified spectator as our baby was sucked out with what looked like a toilet plunger, but went by the far more reassuring name of a Ventouse: 'You push, I'll pull,' the doctor told Tracey, and though the fearful cynic in me thought it would never work, miraculously it did. Jackson appeared. His umbilical cord had been wrapped around his neck, and this had caused the trouble. I had oft been told – by my mother – that I had tried to strangle myself at birth in the same way, and took this to be a sign, a bond between us.

There is a picture of me holding Jackson in the green neon hospital after-glow. It's out of focus, but then it was Tracey who took it, and having just given birth I think a little camera wobble is forgivable. Still, sharp or not, it's a fantastic shot.

Several hours after the event, Tracey packed me off to have some lunch. I stumbled out of the hospital on to the Thames embankment and walked to the Royal Festival Hall, where there was a recently opened posh restaurant. We'd been there once before, when Tracey was heavily pregnant. Now I entered the big glass eatery with its view of the river and its chic staff a changed man: wild-eyed with tiredness, bloated with pride, unwashed and wearing a T-shirt covered with bodily fluids. By way of explanation, I said: 'I'd like a table for one – I've just become a father.'

As I sat there, in a daze, watching my fellow diners and the world go by outside, I realized how relieved I was that it was all over. Birth may be traumatic for the mother, but for the spectating expectant father it can be unbearably anxious-making. I wished in hindsight that I'd demanded to know more about what was going on, that I'd questioned the process, made myself more involved – more responsible. In short, I wished I had been more of a real father – taking charge of a scary situation involving *my* family. But this was idle speculation. The reality of the matter was simple – here I was, toasting my new-born and his heroic mother with a glass of champagne and a meal. I suppose it was the metaphorical equivalent of smoking that fabled cigar, but better, more sociable. I felt that the whole world should know what an extraordinary experience I'd just been through. As I left, the *maître d'* gave me a can of Beamish for Tracey to replenish her iron stocks.

That afternoon there was a bathing lesson in hospital. A nurse asked if we'd like to come and learn how to give Jackson a bath. We followed her to where the demonstration took place, and watched as she delicately washed another couple's new baby. Then it was our turn. Tracey didn't want to, so I volunteered. I made a bit of a mess of it, but Jackson came through, and afterwards I felt an extraordinary sense of achievement. That night I went home, well pleased with myself, while Tracey stayed in hospital. I slept soundly and deeply. The following morning I went to collect mother and son and was surprised and upset to find Tracey pale and on edge, having spent her second night awake. Jackson hadn't really slept, so neither had she. I determined that she would get some rest that evening.

When the three of us were finally alone, at home, I realized that this was it. The meal the day before, the adventure of the bath, let alone the trauma of the birth – it all seemed like some strange game we'd been playing. But this was *it*. Back home, everything was just as we'd left it, same furniture, same dishes, same bedclothes. Only now it was someone else's home too. And we were about to start our new lives together. The previous day I'd been overwhelmed by a sense of relief that it was all over. Now I realized that it was just about to begin.

As you might expect of one who grew up too fast, I was never very good with children. They just seemed, well, so *young*. How were you supposed to talk to them? What did you *do* with them? In recent years, on those occasions when I'd found myself in the company of my friends' toddlers, I'd realized how self-conscious I was when speaking to them – an awkward mixture of patronizing concern and feigned enthusiasm. Now I had my own child. How would I behave?

Our first night at home, I sent Tracey off to bed and took Jackson down to the kitchen in the basement. I wanted to put as much physical distance between us and Tracey as possible, so she'd get a chance to have some rest. This, I thought, was my fatherly duty. I shut the door to the kitchen and, suddenly, Jackson and I were alone for the first time. He was so small, his warm six and a half pounds could fit into the crook of one arm. I walked with him slowly, up and down, trying to settle him. It was dark outside and the lights were off. I sang half-remembered nursery rhymes and I talked to him. Not patronizing now. Just straight and honest. I can't remember what I said, or if I said anything at all – I may just have been having an internal monologue while I sang. But what I do remember is the feeling of those few hours.

It was quite unlike anything I had ever experienced before. Yes, I felt responsible for the creature in my arms. Yes, I felt I loved him unconditionally – though I didn't know him at all, I loved and liked him and wanted the world for him. Yes, I felt fearful of the big bad place I'd brought him into. Yes, I felt protective, proud, strong and immensely important and humble all at once. I felt all these things. But I also felt like a father.

And what does a father feel like? Well, as I write, it's some fourteen months since that night and I'm still learning. Essentially though, I think there is a central paradox to fatherhood. For me, Jackson's birth marked the point at which I felt truly grown up. But, at the same time, it signified a close encounter with childhood – not his, but mine. Most parents, I think, find that they are able to revisit their childhoods through their children's. The toys and songs and games help to recreate an atmosphere of play and wonder, and you do start to look at the world with refreshed vigour. This second childhood, I believe, serves a very important purpose – it helps you cope with the feeling of true adult responsibility and the scary realization that there are no rules, that you're making it up as you go along. Just like a child.

Having Jackson has allowed me to admit that what I considered to be my premature adulthood was in fact a sham – the gloss of being grown up without the substance. He is helping me grow up now, teaching me, through experience, what it is to be a father: what it is to *have* a father. I didn't know before; all I had was a picture culled from my mother's tales and embroidered by my imagination. It was Wordsworth who said, 'The Child is father of the Man'. I think I'm beginning to grasp what he meant.

Jackson and I get along fine. He is just a boy and I am just his dad. I am discovering that the father-child relationship is both ordinary and extraordinary at the same time. The bond is deep – deeper than I can express – and the love I feel for him is like a physical ache. He makes me laugh, and I feel through him that the world can be a wonderful place. I also feel for the first time that I understand what the man who wrote the letter to *Arena* about the male-bonding article meant. Since Jackson's birth I have felt more at ease with other men – dads or not. Bonding with my son has had repercussions beyond our very intimate, personal relationship.

And now when I think of my own father, I see a man and not a myth. He has met his grandson and we are in touch. But when I'm out in the park with Jackson, chasing pigeons, or in Sainsbury's trying to distract him with a bag of Hula-Hoops, or reading him *Dog Is Thirsty* for the six thousandth time, or getting soaked at bath time as he discovers he can splash for England, I sometimes think of my father and I feel sad. Not for me and my lost childhood, but for him and his.

My father's father died when he was young – about fourteen – and some of his subsequent behaviour, the continual questing, for example, seems painfully familiar to me as the mark of a boy who was forced to grow up too fast. He could have had a renaissance with me, but he didn't. He could have had one with his other children too: he did remarry – the woman he had the affair with – and they had five kids. I now know my four half-sisters and my half-brother, and it appears that their relationship with my father was not that much different from mine. He was working a lot of the time and eventually he left altogether. My father chose to have children but not to be a father. I don't blame him for this. I think it was his loss.

So how does a father feel? Tired, certainly. Harassed, probably. Scared, sometimes. Satisfied, absolutely. And yes, very, very grown up.

Stephen Bayley

Stephen Bayley came to
fatherhood as late as he left
childhood. When not tidying up
after the children, he runs his own
design consultancy. When not
running his design consultancy, he
writes. His last book was called
Taste, although he prefers the one
before called *Sex, Drink and Fast
Cars*. He lives in a large, airy and
extremely tidy house in
Kennington with his wife Flo, a
graphic designer and illustrator,
son Bruno, and daughter Coco,
aesthetic terrorists.

Parent Aesthetics

Stephen Bayley finds that
children redesign your life

I can see a drab B52, only five engines remaining, with a bite mark
in the vertical stabilizer. There's a baseball glove and a one forty-
third scale partly completed metal kit of a Ferrari Testa Rossa. Also
on the floor are some dead bugs in various stages of dismantlement
and decomposition from the lepidoptery department of Émile
Deyrolle, the famous Parisian taxidermist on the rue du Bac. There
are installation disks for flight simulator software, a worn-out fluffy
orang-utan called Edward, a badly chewed stuffed lion called Robert
and a bald teddy called The No-Frills Bear.

You get a glossy black adult crash helmet and a wicker basket full
of mismatching hand-me-down Doc Martens. Oh, yes, and a model
Citroën Light Fifteen on top of a paint-stained Apple Mac
PowerBook. A defunct walkie-talkie and two battered radio-cassette
players, one spewing an intestinal mess of mangled tape. A goalkeeper's glove, a nylon rucksack, a tent, an A3 portfolio, a pair of wet
swimming trunks, a broken umbrella, a Fokker DV11, a pair of shin
pads, an old *Lion* annual of mine (1964), a gym bag, thirty-seven
cassettes and some torn Monopoly money. That's it for now as far as
my son's bedroom goes, but I am only talking about the floor.

Moving next door, I'm tripped up by a fluorescent green cat's cradle triangulating the room. There's a rumpled duvet, a Butthead game with crucial parts missing and a three-legged antique chair resting on its side. I can see two tennis racquets and seven different pairs of shoes, not including two pairs of football boots boasting Pompeian accretions of dried mud. The wastepaper basket is inverted and an innocent set of Lego is mixed up with the darkly psychotic miniature figures of a Warhammer game. Carefully preserved is a shredded black bin-bag, a memento of a theatrical performance requiring a chorus dressed as 'Pollution'. There's a Breton *pul marin* and a flannel, a broken goose-necked lamp, a school bag, a plastic coat, some leopardskin leggings, an authentic US Navy cap with the legend USS John F. Kennedy CV-67, a Calvin Klein T-shirt and a single rollerblade. That's it for my daughter's floor. She's nine.

The issue they never raise when you're about to have children is the aesthetic one. People customarily give warnings about the depredations which children make on your budget (vast), your privacy (consistent), your time (total) and your reserves of frivolity (complete loss of), but no one seems to mention the utter trashing they dole out to your sense of beauty, at least as it's demonstrated in domestic order. For the fastidious aesthete the arrival of children is an apocalyptic event, one that calls into question many of life's hard-won assumptions. The expense is manageable, the intrusion on your privacy and demands on your time trivial grievances when weighed against the life-enhancing profundity of parenthood and, in my case, I had so much frivolity there was some to spare. But finding a bit of desiccated orange peel or an attenuated Kleenex or an arm of Action Man or a sticky and fluffy Calpol spoon craftily secreted behind an armoire puts me into spasm.

Since my wife shares my belief that the exterior condition of things is perfectly eloquent of interior states, we started out with some ground rules for how to accommodate children in a house whose visual austerity was such that many unsuspecting visitors used to ask rather pityingly when the furniture was going to arrive. We bought the big Kennington house two years before Bruno was born. Previously it had been in what estate agents politely call 'multiple occupancy', or more plainly it was eleven bedsits with decorative schemes which were correspondingly eclectic. A psychic rush towards neatness had us painting the entire interior an unremitting Antarctic white, but we were slow with other fixtures and fittings. I remember explaining, with what I now see as ridiculous pomposity, that we would not have children until we had bought stair carpet. It wasn't that I put a higher value on a hundred metres of all-wool Axminster than on the launch of my dynasty, it was simply that we were indecisive about the colour and were determined that our first child should be brought up in surroundings that were as neat, elegant and well thought out as we could make them.

In the end we decided on a sensitive shade of pink, a colour that photographed beautifully and would have lasted well enough had all our visitors been steam-cleaned on arrival and issued with bleached calico overshoes, but was inadequate to sustain much abuse from a baby buggy that had been wheeled through damp south London grime by a fussing Yorkshire nanny, who backed up the tyre tracks with size forty-five wellington footprints and a powerful disdain for design-guru uppityness, supported vocally and practically by first our son and then our daughter. It was not long before the bright pink, so reminiscent of a glass of rosé on a summer's day, acquired the coloration and sheen of a flamingo roadkill.

Other rules included a proscription on toys being abandoned in areas conceptually dedicated to adult R & R, since few things are more disruptive of reverie than to see a garish play-pen or a trike through the bottom of your glass of Chardonnay. This instruction I've managed to impose more or less successfully for eleven years with the dual consequence that, while it is possible to sling yourself with confidence into one of our over-stuffed sofas without (much) risk of being impaled on a fragment of a broken Postman Pat van, it has cultivated a taste for aesthetic anarchy whose expression, thwarted in the drawing room, dining room, kitchen and library, has forever been the rolling thunder of creative untidiness outlined in the opening paragraphs.

The aesthetic impact of children extends, quite naturally, beyond the home and into travel. I'd always had two-door cars, a statement of something or other which I held dear, and had promised only to go to four when I joined a golf club, something which I had no plans to do. Still, in a gesture of pre-natal responsibility, shortly after the stair carpet decision, I traded in a sleek sportscar and bought the largest boot attached to a four-door car that my budget could acquire in 1985. This was an Audi 100, an aerodynamic space ship in shimmering silver with a cabin designed to hold five fat Germans, and a boot capacious enough to carry all the luggage they would need for three weeks of golf and twice-daily changes of leisure suits in Torremolinos. It wasn't nearly big enough.

We'd previously travelled carrying not much more than a

Veronelli, a Gault-Millau and a credit card, so anticipated no practical problems when the baby and his nanny were loaded into our vast new car for a summer trip to central Italy. Only those who have never had the experience will be surprised to learn that an eighteen-inch-long 'bimbo di tre mesi' requires the entire boot of a five-seater car for his own purposes. Not only is the list of standard equipment lengthy – at least two bumper packs of disposable nappies, Anglo-Saxon foodstuffs, water sterilizing kit, buggy, collapsible cot, anti-allergenic duvet, sun creams, clothes, toys, a Moses basket – but baby paraphernalia also consumes irrational amounts of space. That collapsible cot weighs little, but its hinged arms, legs and stays are articulated in a way that, even when folded, defines in its awkward-ness a vast volume and denies access to that volume to anything more bulky than a folded newspaper. A fortune awaits the first manufacturer to offer modular fitted baby equipment whose design acknowledges the constraints and irrationalities of car boots.

So we still found ourselves travelling with not much more than a guide book and some slim financial instruments. But how the hotel arrangements had changed too! Travelling as a couple it had always been a delicious existential act to proceed without booking and if, say, Monteriggioni was full then we might get a bed in Radicofani and if we couldn't, we could always sleep in the car or in a field and so what? And when we found our hotel, whatever it was, there was an immediate familiar and selfish acclimatization routine of bath, terrace, wine and any other whim that took our minds or bodies, in whatever order, it didn't matter.

But now, of course, it does. What in 1984 had been a couple in a coupé, was translated the following year into parents in a saloon car with a nanny and a baby and an itinerary to shame a Wehrmacht logistics officer. No one, absolutely no one, who has driven the Ligurian coast road in a heatwave with a howling infant, sweaty nanny and tight-lipped wife would ever, under any circumstances, neglect to pre-book hotel rooms. Chance, poetic discoveries of hotels and restaurants had been replaced by a grimly pedantic sequence of pre-arranged bookings and, instead of leaping up the stairs a couple of risers at a time on arrival to whatever sequence of pleasures circumstance offered up, there was now the more prosaic business of moving two bumper packs of disposable nappies, Anglo-Saxon foodstuffs, water sterilizing kit, buggy, collapsible cot, anti-allergenic duvet, sun creams, clothes, toys and Moses basket indoors from Audi to albergo. This we have done from Calais to Calabria.

The aesthetic impact of children on the arrangements of a well-ordered hedonist is total, but not – of course – wholly unwelcome. It's all part of the trade you make: on the one hand you lose that infinite capacity for selfishness which, you can't help noticing, grows exponentially with childless couples; on the other you acquire a set of responsibilities which, momentarily fatiguing, are in fact the most pleasurable contract you can make; one which binds scruffy old you and the here-and-now to a future well beyond your bus pass. Children give you that sense of otherness that any parent can recognize. There's no mistaking a parent: broke, weary, prematurely aged, but entirely without that febrile preciousness, that ugly involvement with self, which to a parent makes another adult without a child into what's almost another species, or at least people who live by a different book.

I can't think of any better example of how the joyful burdens, fears and responsibilities of parenthood impinge on personal pleasure than a recent lunch I had with an old friend whose children attend the same school as mine. Scheduled to appear at a school open day that afternoon, we decided to tear our pleasures with rough strife through the gates of a newly opened and conveniently located Battersea restaurant. It was summery so we had a kir and joshed while we read the menu, thinking what very fine fellows we were, able to enjoy ourselves in such sophisticated surroundings while still meeting the letter and the spirit of parental duty, being in sight of the school whose agreeably aged red-brick walls were a pleasing symbol of protectiveness. We ordered, perhaps, a little onion tart with rocket salad to start, a bottle of St Veran, sparkling water and a sea bass baked in salt.

About halfway through the excellent onion tart we heard a noise that, commonplace to those without children, every parent hears with scalp-itching dread: the approach of a siren, now howling, now yelping. With forks in mid-air we both saw an ambulance screech down the dedicated one-way street that served our school. The fidgety parent in us strained with anxiety, while the resident aesthete argued for composure. The dispute did not take long. We didn't actually say a word, but as one we got up and rushed from the restaurant just to check the destination of the ambulance. It was long out of sight by the time we reached the school gates, and we returned to our table to enjoy a double dose of smugness together with the fish. Raising a glass or two of the grassy Mâconnais we congratulated each other on our senses of probity and responsibility, and quietly thought how inexplicable it would have been if a mad axeman had been at work, while we toyed, unreflectingly, with the entrée.

Aesthetic arrangements of any sort, from interior design to lunch, are forever compromised by the arrival of children. Children are bad with details and space. Clutter does not impinge on them and, in a sixty-foot drawing room all but empty, my daughter will cheerfully arrange to stand on my toes. But I'm really seriously proud to say we've never had a problem with fridge magnets, although my daughter reserves the right to wind me up with satisfying regularity by leaving a half-chewed piece of fruit, or a football card, or a dirty sock in a nook at the back of our car. She provided us too with the most memorable line from last summer's holiday, when our son said to me, 'God, Daddums, Coco's just spat in the air conditioning!' There you have it.

It's all a bit of a worry, this nice and total disregard for the adult's aesthetic, his details and his space. It's a worry that's not going to go away until I tread that wretched stair carpet for the last time myself. Oh, I forgot to say that it's no longer pink. We capitulated ages ago and changed it to dark grey.

Martin Rowson

Martin Rowson's cartoons
appear regularly in the *Guardian*,
the *Observer*, *Time Out*,
the *Independent on Sunday*,
Tribune, the *Daily Mirror* and
Arena. His latest book is a
comic-book version of Laurence
Sterne's *Tristram Shandy*. He is
married with two children and
lives in south-east London.

BEDTIME STORY

Martin Rowson on the Uses of Literacy.

Tim Dowling

Tim Dowling was born in 1963
in Norwalk, Connecticut. He is
a graduate of Brien McMahon
High School and Middlebury
College. A contributing
editor to *GQ* magazine,
Dowling also writes regularly
for the *Sunday Telegraph*.
His cartoons have appeared in
the *Observer* and the
Spectator. He lives in London
with his wife and son Barnaby.

Boyzone

Tim Dowling on fathers
and sons

As the first item on a long list of apologies to my son I'm preparing for his twenty-first birthday, I would like to say I'm sorry for wishing he was a girl. Of course I don't wish it any more; I haven't since he was born, really, but back in those months before his arrival I not only wished for a girl, I became convinced that I was going to get one. I'm not sure how this happened. I certainly wasn't swayed by the load of weird folklore his mother trotted out about the size of her belly, the food groups encompassed by her cravings or the rhythmic, insistent kicking the foetus got up to whenever she passed a Jigsaw window, all allegedly pointing to the fact that our impending child was going to be female. I knew this was rubbish, and I said so. I pointed out that Jigsaw does some very nice men's shirts. But it was our first child, and there's always a bit of superstition attached to such a momentous event. If my wife allowed herself to be persuaded by a bunch of old wives' tales, I let my wish for a girl become, over time, a conviction.

To me, the idea of having a girl seemed marginally less terrifying than having a boy. Fathers and daughters seem to get on more easily than fathers and sons. For one thing, daughters, in my experience, hardly ever seem to realize what pillocks their dads are, while sons hardly ever seem to realize anything else. Let the rest of the expectant fathers pray for a firstborn son. I wanted a girl and, luckily for me, we were having one.

It's odd how completely surprised you can be by one of two equally likely outcomes. In the end I was no more prepared for a boy than I was for a full-sized, uniformed bus conductor. But there he was, purple, broad-shouldered, barrel-chested and understandably angry. Clearly the name we had settled on was unsuitable. He was nothing like a Martha. I was taken aback, and I fear this may have started our father/son relationship off on the wrong foot.

In fact our father/son relationship didn't even start right away. First he fell asleep. When he woke up, Barnaby (as we had hastily named him while he was unconscious) launched into an almost exclusive relationship with his mother. The first three months were, quite frankly, a cinch. In its early stages fatherhood seems to be mostly legwork, easy enough to handle as long as you're willing to put in the hours. I ran a few errands, changed a few nappies, earned a little money and did a little light housework. Occasionally I was called upon to be a stand-in face for focus practice. I had plenty of time to prepare for our real father/son relationship once it started, although I used up most of that time brooding about my imminent failure.

Changing nappies is fine for now, I thought, but eventually he'll need the kind of guidance and leadership that can only really come from a grown-up. Will I have to hire someone? I'm willing to learn, but there may not be time. I supposed I could probably start the boy off all right. Provided I didn't have to teach him to play ice hockey or anything. I reckoned I could father him more or less effectively right up to the brink of puberty before I'd have to say, 'This is where it all started to go wrong for me. You're on your own from here, son.' As far as being a father to a teenage son, I had no clue. Whenever I thought about it I pictured myself as an alarming composite of Willy Loman in *Death of a Salesman* and the cry-baby in the apron that James Dean is so ashamed of in *Rebel Without a Cause*.

Perhaps my example would be enough to lead the boy to manhood, but it didn't seem to me that my example was particularly exemplary. I didn't want my sins visited on any son of mine. In any case, I'm not sure that leading by example works very well. My own father is hard-working, honest and dignified, qualities he, no doubt, would have liked to pass on to me, but all I picked up was his habit of clearing his throat all the time. I suppose it's still something we can do together. What will Barnaby inherit from me, I wonder? My appalling telephone manner, maybe, or perhaps the athlete's foot, which is the other thing I picked up from my old man. 'Son, this itching, burning sensation has been passed from father to son for generations. Take it and make it your own.'

Even this depressing picture was dependent on our relationship going smoothly for the first eleven or twelve years. By eighteen months there were already problems I hadn't prepared for. The unspoken father/son bond that I had been waiting for had failed to materialize. Actually the boy makes no meaningful distinction between the things he requires from his mother or father, except in the sense that he prefers them all to come from his mother. My attention, my ministrations, my acceptance and tacit approval will all do in an emergency, but they are as nothing compared to the briefest recognition of his existence from his mother. I suppose one always thinks of the Oedipus complex as happening to someone else, but here it was, in my own home. Our little family unit is actually a sinister triangle of competition, in which he and I fight for his mother's attention, while his mother and I fight for his attention. I am usually the clear loser in both heats, and I am definitely in overall last place. There is no sense in which anyone is competing for my attention. If anything, the boy's preference for his mother has become more pronounced over time. There is plenty of evidence that my presence actually annoys him. His first complete sentence, coined entirely for my benefit, is a good example. One day, while I was trying to interest him in a toy I was holding and, by extension, me, he suddenly spoke without bothering to look up. He said simply, 'Go away.' There are days when I am not allowed to touch him or enter his personal space. At times he appears to be contemplating a restraining order.

I'm sorry to say I have not reacted to his indifference or his occasional outright hostility with the sophistication you might expect from a really good dad. I immediately and cravenly sink to his level in order to get some attention. I tend to act more like a sibling than a father. While his mother selflessly teaches him the benefits of patience and controlling one's temper, I teach him to say, 'Hulk angry!' while he's destroying the sitting room because he can't have spaghetti for breakfast. Occasionally I take a little cruel pleasure out of the fact that my presence irritates him. I tell myself that I'm just being the elder brother he'll never have, but I'm more like the little brother I've never been: annoying, if ultimately benign, a tiresome fact of life. Whatever our relationship, it will have to do for now, since parenting is out of the question. I can't teach him anything if he won't pay any attention to me, and the idea of me punishing him is laughable since the thought of falling out of my good books doesn't concern him in the slightest. My parenting, such as it is, consists mainly of standing idly by, ready to distract him for short periods, so that his mother can use the bathroom or the telephone. It's basically what rodeo clowns do. Sometimes I hope he's still too young to understand how inept a father I am, but I'm pretty sure he's just too young to say so.

And yet among people who have observed my relationship with the boy, it is generally accepted that I am good with him, although this is often said in the way one talks about an old family dog who doesn't bite even if you pull him around the room by his ears. In this sense I am very good with him. Though I have been sorely tempted, I have never bitten him. I allow him to pull my ears and my hair. I let him poke me in the eye. I allow him to feed me things that he has, to all intents and purposes, already eaten. He sticks things up my nose, he stands on my head, he digs his fingernails into my throat, he bites my chin, and I just let him do it. Needless to say this policy has not done a great deal to foster his respect. I know he looks on my refusal to bite back as a sign of weakness.

Still, we have our good days, despite our torturer/victim relationship, and the fact that his respect for me diminishes hourly. As his second birthday approaches, there have already been signs of real improvement, and we have found some common ground. We like a lot of the same TV programmes. I've discovered that I can make him laugh, albeit by pretending to cause myself harm. Very occasionally the woman for whose affections we compete becomes the object of our conspiratorial ridicule. Considering he appears to need a father about as much as he needs a hole in the head, Barnaby and I actually manage to rub along quite nicely. If I have to put up with the occasional smack in the chops for daring to make eye contact, well, I just smile and silently add another month to the period between his seventeenth birthday and his first driving lesson. I am told by fathers who have been through this already that the boy's hostility will be replaced by an equally intense devotion in six to eight months' time, so I am being patient. It helps, I suppose, that I am absurdly and uncontrollably proud of him, as if everything he does is a reflection on me. I brag about his most dubious achievements. I find myself saying things like, 'They don't make a bigger nappy!' But even in these moments of fatherly satisfaction I find myself worrying about the future, both distant (Will he grow up to be an angry young man some day?) and not-so-distant (They really don't make a bigger nappy).

Still, it will be years yet before I have to field any questions about sport, sex or personal responsibility. I have plenty of time to decide what to do if it turns out I have fathered the school bully or a serial joy-rider. There's no real way to prepare for the future, and I've always felt that parenting, like politics, ought to be a matter of lurching from crisis to crisis. In the end I simply refuse to believe that being a good father is completely beyond me. It is, after all, entry level human relations. Perhaps being a good father is like being a good husband, which I find is simply a matter of reminding my wife from time to time that she could do a whole lot worse.

I'm sure things will go easier with the next child, provided I can convince my wife that we should have another one, and that I will be better behaved the next time around. And of course this time I might get the daughter I longed for, although I confess I'm now apprehensive about the possibility. At least I know where I am with a boy. Relationships between fathers and daughters are no doubt just as fraught with potential conflict, and I'd hate to make a mistake that I'd regret. I keep thinking of Lizzie Borden giving her father that extra whack, just because.

Pat Kane

Pat Kane is a columnist
with the *Herald* in Glasgow,
and writes regularly for the
Guardian, *New Statesman*,
Scotland on Sunday and *Arena*.
He is also singer and lyricist
with the Scottish band
Hue and Cry. His daughter's
first spelling of his name
was 'Dud'. Which says
it all, really.

Pieces

Pat Kane on fathers
and daughters

---

one

I can't make her a narrative, I can't integrate her into a wise and witty sweep, she's too much current history and too much holy wonder, she's right next to me practising her whistle, if she reads this somewhere down the years then I'm sorry, but only fragments are possible. Beads and shells.

two

A square head, had my G. Extracted from some geometric corner of her mother, in some haste and with no respect for flesh or nature, I had watched her brisk weigh-in through the operation-room porthole. Impossible not to try to read her face like any other sentient human's – even though she'd just been in the safest, most trouble-free place we can imagine; a blissed-out little animal, imprinted by no harsh words (yet), no violent spectacles (yet), nothing on her or in her. And I thought I could read – patience. Curiosity. Intelligence. A Nobel prize. Whatever. I beamed tractor beams of hope and love on to her, radiating her with me, as she squiggled bloodily in the nurse's arms, getting to be alive.

J had ordered me to track G's progress from surgery table to baby room, every inch of the one-minute journey. *Make shure she'zz ourz*: her words rose up out of the pethedine, a grip on my wrist like heavy industry. *Make shure, Pat.* The wee one went past me in a plastic blur, vanishing round corners until I stopped, panic subsiding gently, as her tray was wheeled into place in an empty ward. A brassy old Greenock nurse pressed me into a seat – *pit yersel there, son* – and I gazed away, me and the wean, drunk with sight.

I began my relationship with my daughter at that moment in September 1989: and however ludicrous it may sound, however controverted by every bit of psychology and science, there's been a continuity from our very first meeting. We were, and are, fundamentally relaxed in each other's presence. Perhaps that's because when we first met, we were both After The Ordeal: separate and aware, in a public space, subjects assessing each other as objects. While the woman whose titanic efforts had brought us together was being repaired and restored, me and G were just chilling out in Rankin Maternity Hospital. Both of us glad to be alive. But not going over the top about it. Between convulsive blinks that scrunched her face up like a boxer's fist, G locked into my eyes, poring right into the pupil, inviting me in too.

We were, and are, fundamentally similar. Take this child's head. The nurse had left me with some explanation about *bad position* and *it's only temporary*: and it did alarm me for a minute or two that my first child could have immediately auditioned for an Invasion-From-Mars B movie. But when the snub nose and eyebrow arch and obelisk forehead were fully registered, I knew the future: G had her father's cranium for brains. Instantly, I imagined sweeping small schoolchildren before me, as they taunted my brilliantly achieving daughter for her 'big brainy bonce'. She would have the protector I yearned for at school: her top-heavy burden would not be borne alone. Her father would bear a shining shield for her intelligence. All this would come to be. Or maybe I'd just inhaled some of my wife's hallucinatory gas.

In any case, it was a good hour we spent, gripping fingers and jerking limbs and goofily mugging, before mother was together enough to receive her daughter. With eyes like black coat buttons, J cooed psychedelically over the new kid in the shawl. When G slipped gently on to her mother's nipple, I felt a symmetry between us, rather than exclusion from a bond whose intensity I could never imagine. Me and the kid had already hung out: I knew, and know, what I had to be and to do for her, for them both. Vistas of skipping, chuckling partnership were opening up in my head; thousands of investigations into rubble-strewn areas of knowledge were being planned; an entire lexicon of private language and daft patter was already in the production line.

Only one slurred phrase managed to decentre the joy momentarily, to remind me of what had just happened, and of one factor in its irreducible strangeness. *She'zz a wee girl, a wee baby girl* ... Hell. I have a Girl Child. Now, what does that mean?

three

Archaeologist. Vet. Ballerina. Chemist. Gymnast. Writer. Singer. The list so far.

four

Father-daughter theory is hard to come by and, when obtained, even harder to read. Ross D. Parke's *Fatherhood* (Harvard, 1996) pelts you with small-scale study after small-scale study, until the world seems composed of 'extensive studies of 1500 women' and 'observations of fathers at home with 3-month-old infants in Milwaukee'. But as the psychometric pie-charts pile up, I can't avoid the distinct impression that something is awry in father-daughter relations. And that having a son, in addition to a daughter, now terrifies me.

Take Milwaukee dads: according to Professor Parke, they 'visually stimulated' their infant sons much more than their daughters:

looked at them, jousted with them, wanted to bottle feed them more. Yet the fathers did not hold their sons 'close and snugly – they reserve this type of holding for their daughters'. And if you hold your child tight, you don't allow her actively to move, to reach out to touch and be touched, to grip the spinning handles of the objective world. Parke's conclusion is brutal: when fathers express affection for their daughters, but stimulate their sons, this may be 'the earliest form of gender role-typing'. Dad loves his little honey; Dad loves the wee fella. Give us a cuddle: put up your dukes.

Other studies show fathers 'lifting and tossing more with their boy infants than with their girl infants', and how they 'vocalize more to their girls than to their boys'. An examination of an Israeli kibbutz recorded the patterns of visiting parents, measuring the length of time they stayed in the infant house when visiting: fathers stayed longer with their sons than their daughters. Anthropologists are also brought into the indictment. The Kung San of Botswana, a hunting and gathering culture, have fathers spending more time with boys than girls, particularly as the infants grow up. And let's not forget our fellow simians: rhesus monkeys observed in the lab reveal the same distribution of paternal affections. Other dispiriting stats: fathers spank boys more than girls; fathers argue and fight more in front of sons than daughters.

There's more, but I've had enough, thanks. For all the 'more-than-less-than' comparisons above, I know I've been 'both-and' with G. Crunching her with cuddles and giving her high-fives; teaching her politeness in word and deed, and schooling her in whistling and kite-flying. I've roared at J from the shallow depths of spousal anger across the Italian kitchen, while the wee one fries in embarrassment at my shoulder; and I've arranged those daddy-features for a good-night kiss, while my entire body quivers with anger-for-later. We've turned Polly Pocket into an intrepid space archaeologist with Blu-Tack and tubes, and we've cried at *Beauty and the Beast* for the eleventh time (me first, after about ten minutes, her watching, laughing at each glisten). All present and gender-correct.

But if she had been followed by a boy, soon after? I don't know. I don't know. I have my suspicions. But I don't know.

five

'Don't even *think* about it, wee man.' We are all frozen in the poses of manhood, down the back garden: me and the tenement toe-rags. What are they, eight, nine? Bony boys wreathed in Umbro, skin like cream, hair like horse-mane. I know them and their parents well, I've seen them grow from vulnerable midgets to condensed men, I should be friendly and familiar. But I'm here, rigid and bent forward, aiming a finger right at the freckled one's temple: shouting hard, and it's coming from somewhere unprecedented.

What I seem to be doing at the moment is defending little-girlness. Me and G and her cute-egg pals have been playing football. This is the summer of 1996, and football, in coming home, has leapt the gender gap. When three six-year-old girls are piping in unison about 'the boys won't let us do penalties' at your doorstep, the metropolitan deadline must bend. Leave the screen, excavate the stupid red ball that hardly needs helium to float uncontrollably at the merest touch, and head for the tenement commons with these whispering Shearers. Fifteen flailing minutes of role reversal; small price to pay for personal contribution to end of patriarchy, etc., etc.

After ten, this becomes extreme fun, for a multitude of reasons. The girls are terribly excited that a grown-up – a daddy one – is throwing himself brutally on to the grass to catch and miss their footering kicks; and it's weird, almost futuristic, to hear lassies' voices babble about 'good shot' and 'ooh you missed' in the way I once did. In fact it sounds better: the appreciation is warmer, the laughter is more generous. No grim mimesis of the men in green and white, or the background bark of a father who's always been 'two-footed'. G and her twosome are toe-poking a newsagent's ball all over the place, hopping up and down and hugging and doing collapsible cartwheels, and every organ in my body is smiling. Summer moment, perfecto.

Ball skites off a sycamore, and off to where the bad boys are. Who've been listlessly dribbling and doing desultory keepie-uppie while I've been down here, noisily doing the impossible. At one point, mid-contortion to allow yet another goal, I had caught sight of one boy smirking to another in the distance. Who can't read that male contempt? Their inclusion had been attempted, but the girls rebelled most vocally. So tough, you're out of the fun: live with your idiocy.

Ball rests between two boys, and G patters over to get it. Then the world narrows to a focus: the freckle-kid waits till G makes her articulated-lorry manoeuvres round the ball, and draws his foot back to kick the thing away. It's best to admit that my words – which I can hear cannoning off Hyndland's walls, making their way through glass to mothers' kitchens, immobilizing everything: 'don't even *think* about it, wee man' – are a substitute for a quick dash forward, and a hand across his stupid skull. And it works: whatever part of my Coatbridge past has thrust its way into my throat, they've been addressed by an authentic Central Belt male nutter, in lethal mode. He snaps his foot back, meets my hot gaze, scalded: and, bit by bit, everything unfreezes. The girls seem disturbed, unsure. Eventually, they're off to their den, mingling Disney scripts and teacher tales, removing me gently from their loop.

I'm left with this fucking red ball, and walk back upstairs, passing between the two scared boys. Hammering up the stairs so I don't get a chance to hear a single comment. Shutting the door and slumping, totally confused with myself. Looking out of the window as the lads crunch-tackle, bust the net, swear inexpertly, pull each other around till they're a flushed and giggling knot of energy in the dust. Back to the screen: a tough typist.

six

So what can I give my daughter? These things. A love of language: jokes that clunk and splutter like an old bus, sentences that are as complex as the thoughts that generate them, a range of atrocious accents from RP to Cockernee, words that are accurate as scalpels and turbulent as the sea. A love of knowledge: plunging into the banality of objects – a car, a carton, a cartoon – and coming up with working explanations; connecting light wonderings to long, subtle chains of philosophy and science, hoping that one will suddenly fly across the cobblestones, pulled by her own might; battling Barbie with books, cuteness with concepts, everything that might oppress her with everything that can empower her. And a love of love: how artful and ornate affection can be; how there is forgiveness like a sack of gold under the bed, that can pay any debt, buy all the time you need, facilitate bribes and sustain investment; how to make the flame white, yellow, blue, nearly air, sputtering even, but always on, never in danger, never, always.

Tony Parsons

Tony Parsons is a columnist for the *Daily Mirror*, a contributing editor to *Arena* and a regular contributor to BBC2's *Late Review*. His late father was a Dean Martin fan, while his teenage son favours Dr Dre and Snoop. Parsons, an old punk rocker, is nostalgic for the days when songs had no tunes and you couldn't understand the words.

Father's Day

Tony Parsons reflects on the influence of his own dad

Ason is always growing away from you. It doesn't quite happen on the day he is born, but by the time he can write his own name he is well on the way to becoming his own man. Every day of his life your boy is inventing an ever more elaborate private world where you are an outsider. A loving and supportive outsider, perhaps. But an outsider all the same.

By the time your son is in his early teens, you are sometimes aware that your child is now another country – with loves, fears, dreams, achievements and misdemeanours that you can only guess at. But if our sons grow further away from us as the summers die one by one, our fathers grow ever closer.

The morning after Oasis played Earls Court, I discovered an empty bottle of bourbon and a gigantic poster ripped from the side of the venue on my son's bedroom floor. He was fifteen at the time – although it seems like only the day before yesterday that I sat up with him in the wee small hours as his milk teeth pushed through his gums and he screamed the roof off our little flat – and I wondered what I should tell him.

Son, you don't need hard liquor to be a man? Son, you take this poster right back where you found it? Son, when you are intoxicated, don't do anything that you will regret for more than a day? I knew exactly what my dad would have told me. Because he must have told me the same thing ten thousand times.

'Moderation in all things,' my father always said. It was one of his recurring themes. Boy, did it recur. And when I was a roaring Essex teenager and the lager was flowing like tap water or when I was a speeding *NME* hack and the amphetamine sulphate was twelve quid a gram, his message went in one cloth ear and swiftly out the other. But with a son of my own – a smart, tough kid, but one who wants to be Liam Gallagher when he grows up – the message finally made a lot of sense.

And as I stared at that empty bottle of bourbon, at last I understood. When it comes to drink and drugs, we walk a fine line between having fun and fucking up our lives. Moderation in all things. Of course. Almost ten years after my father's death, I finally believe him.

Even though I didn't always listen to my dad – at least not in my late teens and early twenties – I always thought that he was brilliant at being a father. He was so *good* at it. He was the toughest man I ever knew but he never hit me in his life and I respected him more than anyone in the world. I thought that was some feat. I still do.

'Moderation in all things,' wasn't the only homily. But life had a way of ramming home some of his other lessons a bit earlier than the one about knowing when to say no more.

'There's always someone tougher than you are,' he said, and had the decency not to gloat when I took my first serious beating (a torn black eye and a lot of badly bruised pride).

'Any mug can spend it, but it takes a smart man to earn it,' he said, and after I had quickly blown my first serious cheque from my first successful book, he gave me a loan without making me beg. And, now I think of it, without ever asking for the money back.

I see now that the things he tried to tell me were the fragments of truth he had learned over the course of a lifetime. He knew what he was talking about, but for a long time I was too young and too dumb to listen. And now I wish my own son would take on board the few things I know to be true. Yet I know he has to learn them the hard way.

My father was good at being a father. Perhaps it was because he came from one of those huge, sprawling, old-fashioned East End families, and had grown up taking care of younger siblings – family legend recounted how my father went out to work so that his academically brilliant brother could go to Cambridge, an almost unimaginable destination in that neighbourhood at that time.

But, as good as he was at parenting, my father didn't have any secret knowledge about bringing up a son; there was no master plan to follow or strict guidelines to adhere to. When I had a son of my own I discovered how much improvisation there is to being a father. That trusting face thinks you can do anything. But all the while you are winging it.

Although I ignored all his home truths as so much party-pooping (why believe in moderation when the night is young and the girls are pretty and you are sporting a new pair of Gatsby trousers?), I still believed that my dad had a genius for doing the right thing. I didn't realize that there are no rules to bringing up children. If only it were that easy.

What does the good father do when an eleven-year-old decides to stop doing his homework? Do you rant and rave? Or gently persuade? Is it best to talk quietly about the future or to wave a big stick? Who really knows? Who's to say?

And when a teenage boy brings home a girl that would be desperately inappropriate as a wife – or, far worse, a girl that would be all too appropriate as a wife – should a father quietly have a word in his boy's ear? Or should he keep his counsel and hope it fizzles out of its own accord? Give the boy a packet of condoms or show the babe the door? Who knows?

Well, I always thought my father knew. But now I increasingly suspect that he was doing what every father does – making it up as he goes along. And doing a fair bit of praying.

Only now, with a son of my own, do I see the agonies I must have caused him. He was so proud of me going to a grammar school and must have been devastated when I left for a dead-end job as soon as I possibly could. But he told me he thought I was making a mistake and then let me get on with it. The serious business of screwing up my life.

Then there was sex and drugs and rock and roll, there was freelance poverty, there was divorce, there was another baby boy to bring up – but this one wouldn't have the priceless shelter of a nuclear family. Looking back, I feel like not so much a son, more a soap opera. It was a good job he loved me so much.

And I loved him. The problems we had – and he must have profoundly disapproved of most of the moves I made – were softened by the fact that the love he felt was unconditional. Dropped out, dead broke, strung out, knocked up or loaded – I was still his son. And he was still my hero.

Perhaps every father is a hero to their son. But my father was also the real thing. In the cupboard of our living room in our suburban semi there was the Distinguished Service Medal that he had won as a Royal Marine Commando in World War Two. The DSM (officers are awarded the DSO) is the second highest honour in the armed forces. Only the Victoria Cross is higher – a fact that I knew by heart while my contemporaries were trying to remember that C is for cat.

But we were all children of the war. It filled our games and our dreams. If you were a little English boy growing up in the fifties and early sixties, you were steeped in World War Two. Spitfire, Stuka, Hurricane, Lancaster bomber and Bren gun – these names were as familiar as John, Paul, George and Ringo would be very soon. And unvisited places like Normandy, Dunkirk, Anzio and Hiroshima sounded as familiar as Clacton, Yarmouth, Frinton and Brighton.

And Elba – the island where Napoleon had been exiled – that was the most resonant name of all. Because that was where my father's unit – his 'mob', he called them – went on their last raid. That was where dozens of his friends were killed. That was where he won his DSM. That was where his war ended.

He never talked about the war – often he seemed like the only person in the England of that time who didn't talk about it. Everyone in the family was intensely proud of him, and friends and relations were always reminding me that he was someone special. He rarely mentioned it, and then only to talk about one day visiting the graves of his friends who had died (eighteen, nineteen, they had been – not old enough to vote). But when he took off his shirt, you were reminded of his past because you could see that one side of his upper torso was a mass of scar tissue. The white skin was pulled tight and lined to the epicentre of the wound, like a starburst of flesh and blood. And there were the black nuggets of shrapnel that slowly pushed their way from his body for all his adult life. And of course there was the medal.

He had stopped being a commando years before I was born, but that was the experience that defined him. All the young men he had seen killed and maimed and burnt – and the lives he had taken – did something to his heart. But it didn't warp it, or make it cruel and empty. It made him impossibly gentle. He wasn't the hardened war veteran of popular fiction and the movies. He quite literally would not hurt a fly. If some wasp or bee or spider strayed into the Parsons' home, my father would gently pick it up and carry it to the garden, where it would be set free. It used to drive me and my mum crazy.

His temper could erupt. And when it did, hard men folded, their legs turned to jelly, their bottle suddenly gone. I saw it a few times – with some cocky swimming pool attendant in the sixties when I was learning to swim, and earlier, with some surly boss who refused to let my mother take a personal call when her father was dying from cancer. His temper always had a good reason to explode. But when it did he was uncontrollable, terrifying. And yet he never laid a finger on my mother or me. That would have been unthinkable for him. He was a violent man who learned to be gentle. A hard man who was sickened by violence.

I didn't understand the love he felt for me and the pride he took in my childish achievements until I had a son of my own. And then I looked at that tiny baby and there was some kind of chemical reaction inside me – here was the most precious and beautiful thing I had ever seen. Here was the best thing that had ever happened to me. And suddenly life had me as its hostage. For ever.

As my son grew, I could understand my father's frustrations. Not having enough time free of the tyranny of work. The disappointment he felt when I turned my back on a good education. And I could understand how he felt to be getting older, to live with that gnawing sense that time is running out. Because until you have a child and see how quickly it grows, you can kid yourself that time will never run out.

Our lives were very different. And in many ways they reflected the differences of the generation who came of age in the forties and the generation who came of age in the seventies. He had the war and rationing. I had peace and affluence. He was born into a depression. I was born into an era of entitlement. For me, there was no doubt that life would go on getting more free, more rich, more satisfying. I can see with my son and his friends that those certainties now seem as ancient as the workhouse and the soup kitchen seemed to me.

But unlike my father and my son, I came of age at a time when anything seemed possible, where everything was there for the taking. When I was twenty I packed my bags and set off round Europe for a few months. And other fathers might have objected but he thought it would do me good. He thought a boy should see the world. 'That's what I did,' he said. 'Except, of course, someone was always shooting at me.'

He was a good enough father not to tell me every time he thought

I was making a mistake. I know he didn't like my taste in girls and, later, women. Or rather, he didn't like it when I brought home some sweet-natured nest-builder in a tank top who he adored and then dumped her for some painted Whore of Babylon who he didn't like. And I did that all the time.

What did he want for me? He wanted stability. He wanted me to find a job that I loved. He didn't want me to throw my life away on the wrong girl, the wrong career, the wrong choices that are so easy to make. And now, as my son brings girls home and considers his career options and looks forward to his life as a man, I find that I want the same things for him. They seem like such pathetically modest ambitions. But as the son becomes the father, you realize how carefully these dreams have to be nurtured.

I don't want my son to knock anyone up. I don't want him to get a dose of the clap – or worse. I don't want him to fall in love with someone who isn't worthy of his love. I don't want him to be stuck in a job he despises. I don't want him to be fat, forty and marooned in a loveless, joyless marriage. I want what my father wanted for me. And I managed to find some of that buried treasure. But not all of it. Who does, Dad?

It broke my father's heart when I divorced. Not for my sake – I think after a while a father has to resign himself to the life his adult son creates – but because he knew what it would mean for my son. That he would grow up in a messy tangle of hurt feelings, distance and bitterness – like every other child of divorced parents. It broke my father's heart, because he knew what I didn't stop to think about until much later – that my divorce meant that my son would not enjoy the same kind of home that I had known.

Different worlds, of course. Growing up, I had one friend whose parents were divorced. But very few of my son's schoolfriends are growing up with both their parents. My dad wouldn't have found that fact reassuring. He would have found it ... 'disgusting' is probably the word he would have chosen. As a teenager – or even older – I would have argued with the blinkered certainty of youth. But I wouldn't argue with him now. Not now.

My father was only with a handful of women in his life. There was the East End beauty queen that my mum displaced. A farmer's daughter in Italy during the war who he sometimes alluded to (when I was about thirteen, my jaw dropped when my dad started babbling to a waiter in fluent Italian). And then monogamy with my mother. Almost fifty years of contentment, staying home and early nights.

My life wasn't like that. I had been with more women than that before I even had a vague idea of what I was doing. And I used to think that he was the one who had missed out. I used to think that I was the lucky one – what with my rock chicks and foreign babes and older women and younger women and all the rest. I thought that I was the one who got the sweet deal while Dad stayed home with Mum. But increasingly, I am not so sure.

We were different men. And I have sometimes thought of myself as an inadequate father – because surely I failed the fundamental test of fatherhood when I chose a woman that I couldn't and wouldn't grow old with. But I always thought of my dad as a great father. He was protective, strong, and I could fall asleep knowing that I would wake up safe and sound. One of the enduring memories of my childhood is sleeping on the back seat of the family car, the lamps of the East End streets and Essex A-roads blurring high above (had we been to see my grandmother or to a pantomime at the Palladium?), then being swaddled in a tartan blanket and carried upstairs to bed. Did my son ever feel that secure? I would like to think so.

My son and I have travelled to New York, Thailand, North Africa and most places in between. We have had adventures. We have had a laugh. But surely being a father is about more than sharing good times. Surely being a father is about giving your son a foundation on which to build a life. I know my father did that. I am not so sure about myself. But then, of course, my job isn't over yet. I suppose it is never really over. Certainly up until my thirtieth birthday I was often a source of worry and anxiety to my father. And I am sure it would have gone on for longer than that, if he had lived.

But we could always talk. Unlike mothers and daughters, fathers and sons can always find something to talk about. There is always football. As a boy, my dad had been a goalkeeper in Dagenham, playing in the same school side as a right back called Alf Ramsey. This was the same neighbourhood that spawned Terry Venables and Jimmy Greaves – and they boast about the North-East!

But the early sixties was too soon for a working-class boy to ascend to the heights of his profession while also keeping his East End vowels. My dad's childhood pal had to lose his Dagenham accent when he started to climb the ladder. And when my father bumped into Alf Ramsey – Sir Alf? perhaps not yet – over Romford dog track, he found a changed man. After elocution lessons, Ramsey had been transformed into a ludicrous, coached oo-more-tea-vicar mock toff. My father came home full of scorn and amusement. And I never forgot it, especially when there were attempts to change my accent.

We moved from Romford – emotionally, still part of the East End – to rural Essex, the first of what would later become a tidal wave of the cockney diaspora. My little country school was shocked to have a genuine, gor-blimey-guvnor artful dodger in their midst. My teachers seriously suggested elocution lessons were for little Tony. And it was the biggest laugh my dad had enjoyed since he bumped into Alf Ramsey over the dogs. He was all for self-made men. But you should never forget where you came from.

Later I met plenty of people – lawyers, journalists, broadcasters – who had modified or changed their accents. Scots, Irish, New Zealanders, Geordies, Scousers, Londoners. And I didn't think it was a disgraceful thing to do. But it was never a possibility for me. My dad wouldn't have allowed it. I passed my eleven plus. But it didn't mean I was better than him. Unlike some working-class parents whose kids make it to university, he never felt left behind. Far from it.

But he was upset when I left school. He was proud of me and finally I understand that pride, the ferocity of it. I understand that the achievements of our children can mean more to us than our own. We want them *to get it right*, as we suspect we never did. And when they do, it is a victory over time, a triumph over the mortality of all flesh.

The father and the son are different men. I pride myself on being able to go anywhere, meet anyone, feel at home anywhere (which is of course the same as feeling at home nowhere). But my father didn't want to belong. He despised the establishment. He loathed authority all his life.

For example, he was a cop hater. The police made his blood boil. When they put on their sirens he insisted they were just 'going home for their bloody tea'. And if he ever got pulled over to the side of the road, he always made it worse by getting lippy. He wasn't one of those good citizens whose legs turn to mush at the sight of a blue uniform. He had a burning hatred of the law, who he accused of being venal, cruel and corrupt. As a child I found it embarrassing. Later I felt he was just making life unnecessarily hard for himself. But by then it was too late to change. And I didn't really want him to change. I liked him the way he was.

But I grew up wondering how I could ever fill his shoes. I grew up in the shadow of his medal. How could I ever compete with that heroism? How could I ever experience anything that intense? How could I ever achieve anything that would be so worthy of respect? I still don't know.

And yet my father lived a very quiet, peaceful life. After the war – which was over by the time he was twenty – he worked on a stall and as a lorry driver. By the time I was born he was a greengrocer and by my teens he was working as a produce manager for a chain of supermarkets, driving around and making sure their stock was good. He had a company car, annual dinners at the Hilton (he looked good in black tie) and was full of complaints about the unions.

When I was growing up, the great debate in the house was if my dad should start his own business. His 'boys' – the fifteen- and sixteen-year-old lads who worked as his minions in the greengrocer's – would frequently go off and try running their own shops. And sometimes they would turn up years later with the Mercedes and the glam wife and the big house with the bar and the pool. And they would grin and slip me a ten shilling note and say they owed it all to my dad.

Yet just as he had resisted attempts to get him to become an officer in the forces, so he resisted efforts to get him to become a businessman in civvy street. But I think he sometimes wished he had. He didn't envy his boys their ulcers or their brushes with the tax man or even their glam wives. But he had a highly developed sense of pride and I think he sometimes regretted not having greater material success. 'We could have been millionaires by now, Em,' he would sometimes wistfully tell my mum. And I remember that wistfulness as I dream of bigger contracts, more money and greater success. I don't ever want to be wistful about missed chances. Perhaps that is my way of living with the medal.

We were a working-class family. For the first five years of my life we lived above a greengrocer's shop in Harold Hill, Essex. Opposite was a patch of wasteland where they later built a bubble gum factory. We continued to live there even when my dad went off to work at a shop in Tottenham.

My father worked long days and he also worked Saturdays. My two memories of the 1966 World Cup Final are saying, '*Fuck*' in front of my mother when the Germans equalized. And the other is that my dad had to work that day, just like every Saturday.

He worked hard. Far harder than me. Yet I often feel like my father must have felt. I wonder what exactly I am working for; I wonder what I am missing; I wonder if it is worth it. And I see in myself his tendency to pull up the drawbridge, to shut out the world, to make his family the centre of the universe.

There was a mystery about him. Once, between greengrocer jobs, he worked in a warehouse that was held up by armed men. And one night I discovered two handguns on the back seat of his car. I never mentioned them to him but I suspected that the old commando was ready to shoot back if they came again. An unlucky yob had once walked into his shop in Barking asking for protection money. My father made sure that he never asked again. There was always something dangerous about him. None of the parents of my friends – those stolid home-brewers and golfers and car-washers – had fathers who sometimes left handguns on the back seat. I was proud of him.

We were an ordinary working-class family but we felt special. We felt superior, even, not because of money or accents or social graces or education or any of that. We felt special because of my dad. Because of what he had done. Because of who he was. And because of the medal.

His great love was the sea. He was still the sailor he had been when he entered the armed forces in his mid-teens, and once a year he would go off alone to Cowes, for the sailing. That was the extent of his social life, apart from gatherings with the regiments of brothers, sisters, in-laws and children (who eventually all moved out to our neck of the woods). After his annual escape to Cowes, he would stay home with me and my mum for the rest of the year, tending his garden, laughing at *Morecambe and Wise*, shaking his head at the footage from Vietnam where frightened GIs huddled together in the jungle. 'You should never stand together like that,' said my dad. 'Because all it takes is one grenade.'

He loved his home, but he could be impatient with the trappings of domesticity. I remember one Boxing Day his sister turned the Hoover on in her place and my father swore we would go somewhere else next year. And like him I find myself treating every vacuum cleaner I hear as a personal affront. You can love your home without wanting to hear vacuum cleaners after work. That's how my dad felt. And I agree with him.

He has been dead for nine years now. Lung cancer. I didn't cry at his funeral but I cried when I heard he had a tumour and that it was terminal. But then I had to be strong because I am an only child and it wouldn't have been right to fall to pieces. It is OK to cry, he had taught me. And it is OK to be afraid – only a fool is never afraid. But being a man also carries certain obligations, certain duties, certain responsibilities. He drummed that into me and I am glad that he did.

He had known about the cancer for a year or so, I reckon. But he kept it to himself. So when he collapsed and was rushed into hospital, yes, it was a shock. But it was all over in a few weeks, which made it easier for me and my mother than if it had dragged on for a year. Which of course is exactly how the old boy had planned it.

He faced up to the knowledge of what was growing inside him, the thing that would kill him at sixty-two, and he kept it to himself to protect those around him. In the hospital, full of morphine, I could see he was frightened – of course he was frightened – but he was still the bravest man I had ever known. I spent my childhood pretending to be a hero. My father was the real thing.

They say that headstones need special cleaning every ten years or so. And recently my mother went into the undertakers to enquire about having the headstone cleaned.

'Name of the deceased?' the undertaker asked her.

'Victor William Robert Parsons,' said my mother. 'DSM.'

'That shouldn't be hard to find,' the undertaker said. 'I shouldn't think there are too many DSMs over there.'

'No,' said my mother. 'I shouldn't think so.'

My father's life was always unimaginable to me. I couldn't imagine those war experiences. I couldn't imagine what it was like to love one woman for a lifetime. And I couldn't imagine what it was like to be him.

Yet I look at my son's uncharted future with my father's eyes. What if you can't get a job? What if she gets pregnant? What if you stop loving her? What if she stops loving you? What if you're not happy?

The son laughs with his friends and watches the girls go by, while the father's lot is pride, fear, frustration, protectiveness and a profound love for someone who is both an extension of himself and yet very much his own person. The father and the son. One flesh. Two lives. And the son has absolutely no idea of what the father is going through until he becomes a father himself. Finally you see with the eyes of the ages.

My father taught me how to be a man and he taught me how to love. And I think that if I can leave my son an inheritance like that, then I will have done my job as a father.

Carlo Gébler

Carlo Gébler was born in Dublin in 1954, and now lives in Enniskillen. His day job is teaching (part-time) in HMP Maze. He is the author of novels (most recently *The Cure*), short stories (most recently 'W9 & Other Lives'), journalism, articles, scripts and criticism. He is also an occasional director of documentary films; the last was *Baseball in Irish History*, a film about punishment beatings in Northern Ireland. He is currently judging the *Irish Times* International Fiction Award, and writes a column for *Fortnight Magazine* in Belfast.

My Life as a Stepfather

Carlo Gébler describes his
very special inheritance

In those days I lived in a flat in Little Venice rented from the Church Commissioners; top floor, two very large white rooms. It was a summer's day, the windows were thrown open and in the communal gardens, three floors down, sprinklers turned with a soft hiss.

'I have a friend you'd just love,' said Anna, moving the ice in her glass. 'Trouble is, she's getting married.'

Anna was German, and her intonation was, yes, a little like Marlene Dietrich.

I can't remember why she came out with this remark, but I am certain it was not a taunt, simply a statement. She knew me; she knew Tyga; she knew we would fit hand in glove; but Tyga was marrying someone else, so, *tant pis*, that was that.

Dissolve to six months later. Anna was giving a party in a large flat in South Kensington. I remember a vast room and pine floorboards. A girl was dancing with abandon. A stripper having a night off, someone explained. A middle-aged female hippie with long grey hair, dressed in a buckskin suit, a Davy Crockett hat and carrying a shaman's wand, moved on to the floor and started to dance with the girl. The guests watched, waiting for something to happen. For a minute or two it was interesting. After twenty minutes, less so. I decided to leave. As I went to get my coat, I glimpsed a woman with black hair and coal-black eyes; she was wearing a green skirt that rustled as she moved. We had not been introduced but I knew this was Tyga, and I saw right away that Anna was right.

It was February, the following year. London was cold and gloomy. I invited Anna to come over with her boyfriend to play Scrabble. They were invited for eight.

At six, Anna was on the phone.

Did I remember Tyga, the one she had told me about?

Of course I did.

Then Anna told me the story.

Tyga had got pregnant and in January, just a month earlier, she had married the father. She'd lived with him for years and they had always intended to marry. He was an artist, a much older man, divorced, and he had a child by his first wife. Anna had been to the wedding.

Then, continued Anna, six days after the wedding, Tyga's husband suffered a massive heart attack while he was driving. He died shortly afterwards.

I can't remember what I said.

Anyway, continued Anna, Tyga, the widow, twenty-four, pregnant and grief-stricken, was now staying with her and her boyfriend – for understandable reasons Tyga didn't want to go back to the flat where she had lived with her husband for six years – and Anna's question was, could they bring her? I was adamant; they had to bring her. Four was a much better number for Scrabble than three.

At eight the bell rang and I pressed the buzzer. I heard footsteps on the stairs and my own front door opening. I turned and saw Tyga for the second time; same dark skin, same coal-black eyes, but her expression was one of heightened anxiety. She looked to me like someone who thought a terrible creature was lurking, waiting there to pounce on her.

We started the Scrabble game, playing on the floor. Tyga was opposite me. We may even have partnered one another. I can't remember. All that sticks in my memory is that every so often she went to the bathroom and returned after a moment or two having applied a new coat of lipstick.

We started to see one another, socially. Then it was St Patrick's night and she came round to the flat. The Irish are in luck tonight, I thought. We went to bed. Her stomach was a hard, small, round, about half the size of a football.

We began an affair but it didn't last long. One Sunday morning,

Tyga came bearing a white box filled with éclairs from the local pâtis-
serie. A propitiatory offering. She told me she was not ready for a
relationship so soon after her husband's death. She told me this was
to be expected; after all, she was carrying his baby. She told me that
our relationship was too complicated and too fraught. I did not like
what I heard because I was in love. We parted badly.

September came and the first leaves were burnt in the communal
garden below the flat. One evening, my friend Aziz and I were sitting
at my glass-topped table, talking and doing lines of coke and drinking wine, when the telephone went. It was Anna with the news that
Tyga had just given birth to a perfect little girl.

Aziz was a small, wiry Egyptian; he was one of my closest friends.
News of the birth stirred him deeply. He pulled a ring off his finger;
it was a gold ring with a large red stone set in the middle; he
declared that we must now go to the hospital, he and I, immediately,
and present the new-born infant with this gift. I demurred. It was a
terrifying thought; the idea of the two of us waltzing around Queen
Charlotte's Hospital in the middle of the night, coked up to the
eyeballs, and locating both the new-born baby and the exhausted
mother, then presenting our gift. I said something about it being
too late.

Aziz said we had to go. It was our duty, he said. He supported his
case with quotations from the Koran and references to ancient Islamic
tradition. I said I was too drunk to drive. He said we would go by taxi. I
think then I told him the truth. Or he guessed it. I was in love with the
mother, I said, and given the stimulants in my system, I would probably end up looking stupid. Aziz made me take the ring anyway, made
me wrap it in tissue paper and put it away in a drawer.

I handed the gift over, as I had promised Aziz I would do, when I
went to see Tyga the next day. Then I went and peeped at the new,
small, blond baby lying in a Moses basket, wrapped in a blanket. The
name of the child was India. And what did I feel? Well, the answer
was nothing, really. Not at that moment. All I saw was a baby. I knew
about the baby's unhappy circumstances; I knew it was a baby who
didn't have a father; but for me it was just a baby, a small thing that
cried, ate and slept, in that order, nothing more. I did not find the
sight of new life thrilling, and I certainly did not understand the
mother's desire for her pride and joy to be celebrated.

My not understanding this particular need came to the fore the next
week when Tyga suggested a walk. I thought it would be a great
opportunity for us to talk.

We walked down the Goldhawk Road and turned into Ravenscourt Park. Of course I'd got it completely wrong. The mother didn't want to talk; what she wanted was to show off her child; and what she also wanted from me was a hint, at the very least, of fatherly or masculine pride; after all, she had just brought a new life into the world. If I'd stopped to think, perhaps it would have been obvious that now, so soon after India's birth, and with her husband dead, this is what a widowed mother would crave. If her husband had been around, he'd have let everyone know he was with a new child, his child, and how proud he was. But I didn't stop to think. I just walked and talked; Tyga grew silent, which I interpreted as grumpiness, and India slept sweetly under her covers.

Despite this disastrous excursion to the park, and despite other similar experiences, when we were together but wanting completely different things from each other, our friendship, our attachment to one another, never quite died. We never did anything terrible enough to kill it off.

Consequently, over the years that followed, during which we each had other relationships, we would always see one another a couple of times a year. Our meetings were never amorous but always cordial, and on each occasion I would find India a little older, a little bigger. While she lay in her Moses basket and gurgled, or later, while she played with her Fisher-Price tea set or her dolls, her mother and I would talk. Neither of us said much – that is to say, neither of us said anything of importance – but when we parted there was always a shared sense that under the crust of the conversation, deep and powerful feelings were moving around and waiting to get out.

Four years on, our relations became amorous again. After a while we decided to live together. One morning Tyga appeared outside my flat in her rusting Fiesta. She was wearing a bright African skirt. I carried her boxes of plates and saucepans and kitchen utensils up to the flat. But she was not moving in completely. We had agreed on a trial period. She was keeping her flat in Shepherd's Bush. There was her daughter to think of. What if she gave up her flat and our relationship collapsed? I agreed. Absolutely.

India was five when her mother came to live with me. I didn't know anything about children. Nor had I, until I met Tyga, ever (at least consciously) imagined that my life was going to involve children. I know the psychological explanation can only ever be partial, but my parents' painful and protracted divorce had induced a queasy distaste on my part for the whole business of procreation in relationships. Marriage and children, in my experience, only produced unhappiness.

However, I should stress that my views weren't conscious. I hadn't openly rejected children, and I wouldn't have been able to articulate – in those days – what I've said above. It would be more accurate to say that my position on children was this: they were simply not included in the plan. I was going to be a writer and occasionally a director of films. I was going to travel. Then, out of all the women in the world I choose to take up with one who had a child, and now, suddenly, the child was in my home, and my life as a stepfather was about to start.

Well, not immediately. To begin with I was the mother's boyfriend; I was Carlo, and India called me Carlo. This went on for several months: Carlo this, Carlo that.

Then, one afternoon, when I was at my desk, Tyga crept up, a silencing finger across her lips. 'Sshh!' she said, and led me to the corridor which connected the two huge rooms that comprised the flat, at one end of which hung a full-length mirror. India was standing in front of the mirror in her tartan dress, her fine blond hair in a ponytail that snaked down her back. A Norman Rockwell painting if ever I saw one.

India was saying something to the mirror. For a second or two I couldn't quite hear what it was, so fast were the words tripping off her tongue. Then my ears adjusted. She was conducting an imaginary conversation, sometimes calling me Carlo, sometimes calling me Dad. As her stream of talk continued, she said Carlo less and less, and Dad more and more. Then her focus became just the word – Dad – and she tried saying it in her happy voice, her sad voice, her loud voice, her commanding voice, her princess voice, her wizard voice, her robot voice and so on. The rehearsal lasted for several minutes, throughout which India was quite unaware we were both watching.

That evening, when she was putting India to bed, I heard Tyga suggesting that she was free to call me whatever she wanted, Dad, Carlo, whatever, and the next morning it was Dad when she woke me up and has been ever since.

My position, I know, was special. Most stepchildren have a living mother or father to whom they can return, or at least refer. India had no such figure. She knew about her father, Mike, of course; knew he was her biological father and that I was her other father; however, there was no living person she could talk about or go to see; that first original father, he was gone. This made the life we started living together much easier than I know has been the experience of other step-parents. There was no figure of whom I could be jealous, no figure she could use to taunt me. There was just us and we had to get on with it.

I did not love India when she appeared in my life, not for herself, I mean. She came into my life because I loved her mother. Then I loved her because I thought I ought to (which was not love) and then because I wanted the mother to love me (which was self-interest). What happened in the years that followed, was that slowly we began to grow into each other. Shared experience between the step-parent and the stepchild is what forges love. It won't necessarily be all good (the experiences, I mean, the love, of course, is always good); also, most of the experiences are minor, domestic and they make poor copy. But there are, as I look back, certain key moments in this process that are big and have narrative weight. On the road which I travelled with India these – for me – are some of the milestones.

The first occurred one summer's afternoon about the same time as she started to call me Dad. India was peering out of the window into the communal garden. The boisterous screeches of children and the lower tones of organizing mothers drifted from below. It was Lawrence's party going on out there. He was one of our neighbours' children. India knew the boy vaguely. He was a couple of years older than her. He had let her play with him a few times when there were no better, older children around, and in her mind that made them friends.

India ran out of the room. I heard her clattering around in her bedroom. She came back wearing her best dress, her best shoes and her best Alice band. I knew what was coming, was already sick about it, and then the words came and confirmed the worst. Would I take her down to the garden to her friend Lawrence's party? she asked. All the other children were out there, all the other children she knew and played with were in the communal garden.

I explained quietly that although what she said was true and she did know Lawrence and several of the guests as well, unfortunately she was not invited, possibly because he was a boy and he was a bit older and he just wanted boys of his age.

She shook her head. It was a children's party. She was a child. Ergo, the party was where she belonged.

I told her I couldn't take her down.

She insisted. Would I please take her down?

I explained to India that it would embarrass Lawrence's mother if I appeared with her. As I explained this, I could see the expression on her face slowly changing from gleeful anticipation to sorrowful acceptance.

I suggested a walk, the park, the shops, I can't remember. India fetched a big chair, dragged it to the window, got up on it. No, she insisted, she was going to watch the party. She didn't move for the rest of the afternoon.

That was my first lesson in fatherhood (at least that I remember consciously). Hurt was inevitable and there was nothing I was going to be able to do. Fatherhood was not only bath time and ice creams and stories, it was also failure. And as I recognized this, I was filled with a hubristic ambition. Never again would the child suffer. At least not at my hands. What I was to learn next was that not only was it impossible to protect her, but that I would also be a cause of hurt (including the heartache that comes with exclusion). I was not and never would be perfect.

At that time I was making a documentary film about the 'notorious' Irish writer, Francis Stuart, who is best known because he spent the war years in Berlin and further blotted his copy book by broadcasting for the *Reichfunk* to Ireland.

Because the subject was 'difficult' the funding of the film was erratic. Over the previous two years, work on the film had started, stopped, restarted, and stopped again. Then, during the first winter India and I were together, Francis Stuart came to London. I decided to give a dinner. I liked him. Also I wanted to keep him committed to the film. This was a big occasion: twenty people, starched tablecloths, a four-course meal.

The guests were assembled. They stood or sat around the big room in my flat, drinking and talking. Suddenly I saw a little face at the door, scrutinizing the room. What was India doing? I wondered. I thought she was in bed. I called her in but she ran off. I heard her feet in the hall. Then, a few moments later, she reappeared, dragging her own small bedroom chair, the one that went with her own small table. She dragged the chair across the floor, manoeuvred it into the space beside the guest of honour, and sat down. That was the moment when I saw that what she wanted, more than anything, was the assurance of a guaranteed place in every situation, and that my first task as a stepfather was always to make her feel included and never to leave her out.

Another memory; the event was small, yet the significance

remains massive. One Sunday, Tyga and I went to the flat below for drinks. When it was time to leave, the host, Jonathan, followed us along his hall towards the door. Suddenly, there was a loud crash overhead. The ceiling shook and the light bulb dangling from the ceiling rose went pop. Three sets of adult eyes swivelled upwards. The crash was India, of course. Her room was directly above Jonathan's hallway. Seven years old now, and gymnastically ambitious, India had taken to jumping and tumbling, somersaulting and cartwheeling in her bedroom.

As we apologized, Jonathan opened the hall cupboard. From floor to ceiling it was filled with boxes of light bulbs. As Jonathan removed the broken bulb and put in a new one, he mentioned that he did this as many as half a dozen times a week if India was being particularly boisterous. We were embarrassed, but our host was blithe. She was a child, of course she was going to break light bulbs. Would I have my daughter any other way? he asked.

'Of course not,' I said, and then it struck me that he'd used the word daughter without saying 'step', and that pulled me up. Jonathan knew about India's circumstances and yet, I realized, as far as he was concerned I was her father. That was the moment I recognized that part of this mysterious bonding process had nothing to do with oneself and everything to do with others and the way they would push you together. The ending of *Gregory's Girl* (when John Gordon Sinclair's mates sort out his love life) might be saccharine but it was also true and that was a cause for joy. I believe I ran straight upstairs and gave India a hug, although she hadn't a clue what this was about.

After living together for nearly two years, we decided, Tyga and I, that we would have another child. A sibling for India. A proof both to her and ourselves that we were committed to being a family, an expanding family. A proof of our love. And Tyga wanted more children. She always had.

Jack was born at home on a sweltering June night, with all the windows thrown open. India was in her room. The midwife went and told her she had a brother. She bounced on her bunk with joy and proclaimed with Freudian gusto that now she had someone to marry. Jack would be her future husband.

Over the weeks that followed, Tyga lay in our bed in a cotton nightdress, suckling the infant and receiving a stream of visitors, and I went into shock. A ready-made fully formed five-year-old had been my first experience of fatherhood. She talked, she walked, she even brushed her own hair. But now, here was a small, helpless ball for whose care I was responsible. For ever.

It occurred to me then, but vaguely, that I had not felt that for India. She had never been a small helpless ball for whom I knew I was responsible. With Jack's birth, I saw that I needed to be more India's father than I was. I'll rephrase that. I saw I hadn't yet taken on board – or as shrinks would say 'internalized' – that inner sense of absolute custodial responsibility. In the case of the weak, mewling infant that was my first-born son, this was obvious; that I was responsible for his creation was inescapable. However, in India's case that word 'step' was still there before the word father (despite all the hugs and all the shared experiences, it wasn't banished) and not until the word was gone would I be for her what it was immediately obvious I was already going to be for my son – the unconditionally loving (though far from perfect) parent. To steal from the child psychologist Bruno Bettelheim – the good enough father.

At the end of the eighties we left London and came to Ireland, to Northern Ireland to be precise, to Enniskillen. This was so I could write a book. It was going to take six months, then twelve months; it ended up taking eighteen months. At some point Tyga discovered that to buy a house would cost half what it was costing to rent a house. So we did, buying an old school set amongst drumlins. Meanwhile, India went to a local primary school; she acquired a Fermanagh accent and developed a loathing for the countryside. Her fantasy was that we should all live in a modern house on one of the satellite estates around Enniskillen.

As she grew older she was obviously developing her own personality, and acquiring aspirations which were not only different from those of her father (and mother); quite often they were in direct conflict. Interestingly, as this was starting to happen, Tyga and I decided to have a second child (perhaps unconsciously we wanted another baby to compensate for the fact that we were losing India). It was a boy, called Finn, and after his arrival quite unexpected anxieties regarding our mortality suddenly began to affect us.

What would happen, we wondered, if we were both to die? I had a brother and a mother to whom the Gébler boys could go. But India was still a Rudston Thomason. We had no contact with her biological father's family, but who was to say, in the event of simultaneous deaths, that India wouldn't be sent to them? Tales of heavy-handed social workers splitting up families of siblings and half-siblings between their respective blood relatives resolved me to adopt.

However, on enquiring, I discovered that the law required that I marry the mother if I wanted to adopt the daughter.

Tyga and I decided, immediately, to marry. Invitations were issued; the banns were published in the *Impartial Reporter*, the local paper. We exchanged vows in the Register Office with the new-born Finn firmly clamped to his mother's breast.

Next the business of the adoption was set in hand. I was assessed by numerous social workers. My GP submitted a report on my mental and physical health. The RUC reported that I did not have a criminal record.

At last the day came. As a family we presented ourselves at the courthouse in Enniskillen. The clerk told us that the final interview with the judge, the one that would make the adoption legal, would not take place in the court, but in judge's chambers. A domestic setting, after all, said the clerk with a smile, was more appropriate, given this was not a criminal matter. Absolutely right, mate.

We followed the official down the steps, then found ourselves in the bowels of the building, walking along a corridor, cells to the right and left of us, all packed with manacled paramilitary prisoners who were shouting at one another and banging their handcuffs on the bars. These twenty men were there because of the things Northern Ireland is famous for; they were there to answer charges for such crimes as conspiracy to cause explosions, causing explosions, murder and membership of an illegal organization. Like us all, India was fascinated, silent and a little unnerved.

The judge was a quiet man sitting behind a large desk. He introduced himself, then explained he needed to ask India a few questions. Did she understand what was happening today? he asked. She shook her head. 'No.' Tyga and I looked at one another in astonishment. We had been preparing for this moment for over a year. India had also had numerous solo interviews with social workers who had gone over this ground. She had understood. She knew what was happening. God damn it! she'd agreed to this. The judge smiled kindly and explained that I was to become her legal father. Then I understood something more of India. (I knew it already but there are some things you have to learn over and over again.) She loved lots of attention.

She explained afterwards, in Scoops Ice Cream Parlour where we took the children for celebratory knickerbocker glories, that with the commotion of the remand prisoners outside, she had felt confused. However, I need not have worried that her 'No' signified unconscious dissent. The following Monday morning she changed her surname on the school roll, and she changed the name on her exercise books when she came home in the evening, and I think, with that, the word 'step' was finally, finally erased.

However, this should not be taken to mean that her biological origins were then consigned to an Orwellian memory hole. On the contrary, we have always thought it important to keep those facts alive. A couple of years ago, unpacking a trunk of Tyga's possessions, we discovered a sketch pad of her father's drawings.

'Oh, wow,' said Jack, a vociferous six-year-old by now, 'are these your dad's drawings, India, or are they our dad's drawings?' by which he meant me.

As the children pored over the drawings, something very important happened, catalysed by Jack's question. Tyga went to the telephone and dialled India's half-brother, Barnaby. The last time she had seen him, Barnaby was fourteen and India was three.

To cut a long story short, that Christmas in London, we went, all of us, to see Barnaby. He was tall, twenty-four, with a ponytail. India, I think, was over-awed by this mythical half-brother in whose presence she now stood. She was silent and tongue-tied. Not so the bold Jack. Within seconds he was up on Barnaby's lap, and within minutes he had Barnaby talking about football.

Children have a gift for plunging on, unfettered by anxieties, unlike us adults. As I watched India watching her wretched little brother hogging her Barnaby's attention, I realized that she was no longer the child I thought she was; she was shading into adolescence.

This story started in a sense with Anna, and how apt that I can bring her back into it. She came out to stay with us in Ireland at the end of the summer. She is married now, with her own children. She came bearing gifts of clothes for ours – we have four now. We had a baby girl in 1994. Georgia, as she is called, and the two boys accepted their presents without demurring, but then India was called forward and there was a moment of anxiety. She is a teenager now and as the parents of adolescents know only too well, they are notoriously hard to judge when it comes to clothes. Would it be right, would it be wrong? In the event the Kookaï skirt was a huge success.

The exchange of gifts was over and wine was opened; meanwhile, I noticed something I had never noticed before (no doubt because of not paying attention). India had the skirt on. She was looking down at the hem and sliding the waistband around her hips. Where had

I seen that before? That exact movement? It was like having a tune on the tip of the tongue, a tune that is maddeningly evasive. Then it came. Of course. That was exactly, exactly what her mother did.

Recently, India had her fifteenth birthday. Her mother was in a state of shock. If the changes between when India was born and now seemed huge, just think, she said, how much greater the changes would seem in another fifteen years hence, at which point India would be thirty. Now she still lived with us, but in fifteen years' time, said my wife, she would be living away from home, she might be married, she might have children, she would not be our little girl any more.

To celebrate the birthday we ordered an Indian take-away (India's idea). She asked for a lamb vindaloo. 'Far too hot,' we said. But our daughter managed it, of course she did, with small beads of perspiration glowing on her forehead, thus offering us yet another sign that the result of this long and unpredictable process called parenting is an autonomous individual who is both everything one is and, at the same time, absolutely unique.

If there is a theme to this piece, it is how surprising, how unexpected this has all been. I never really thought all those years ago before I met Tyga that my life was going to turn out as it has. That I would have four children, and that I would end up living in Northern Ireland. Well, of course I didn't. I didn't know myself, did I?

Yet when I look back I see how clearly others saw then what I have since become (just as I was able to see the trajectory of their lives to which they were blind). There was my friend Adam, for instance, with whom I shared two flats long before any of this happened. One day, out of the blue, he made a prediction: me in the country, rattling around in a stationwagon, kids piled in the back, which is pretty much how life has turned out. If I'd known then what I know now, it might have made the journey here less alarming and I certainly would have wasted less energy trying to kick against the inevitable.

I am not the best parent, but I hope my children will always like me. I know I was harder on India because she was the first than I was on Jack, and that I played less with Jack than I did with Finn, and that I am more impatient with Finn than I ever will be with Georgia, the baby. I think we would all be much better parents if we could treat all our other children as we treat our last-born. If they teach you anything, children teach you to be better to the next one.

David Flusfeder

David Flusfeder was born in 1960.
He lives in London with his wife and
son. His first novel, *Man Kills Woman*,
was published in 1993. His second,
Like Plastic, was published by
Jonathan Cape in 1996.
He has also contributed short
stories and articles to magazines
and newspapers, and has managed
cinemas in New York, projected films
in London, taught Creative Writing at
Pentonville Prison and criticized
television for *The Times*. He is
currently writing his third novel,
contemplating having another child,
and translating the work of a poet
from the Warsaw Ghetto.

The Shrine

David Flusfeder on every father's worst nightmare

When our son Julius was seven months old we walked him over to the doctor's because his right ear seemed suddenly to be pushed forward from the side of his head. One unreal hour later we were all at the hospital; the diagnosis of mastoiditis had been made; and Julius was receiving buckets of antibiotics through a drip tube that had been tapped into the side of his foot.

I don't like hospitals. My mother died in one and even though my son was later born in a different one, that wasn't enough to tip the balance. I still see them as death places rather than life places. And here was Julius, lying in a large iron bed that made him appear poignantly small. He was slightly feverish, and very tired, but still with a keen look of curiosity for the world around him and a clear, pleasant, hopeful trust that this was a good place, that nothing bad could happen to him here.

Mastoiditis is the inflammation of the mastoid bone of the skull behind the ear. The consultant was agreeably surprised to see it. As if he were just meeting an old schoolfriend of his father's for the first time.

— Mastoiditis hardly appears any more. They used to get a lot of it before the war. It's a disease associated with – excuse me – poverty and malnutrition. I was told about a case a few months ago. Indian family.

— That's very interesting, we lied, but what can mastoiditis lead to?

— It's an inflammation, said the consultant. A local infection.

— We understand that, we said, but everyone's so worried. What are you all worried about?

— Antibiotics will do the trick. Don't worry. We got to it in time. If we hadn't we'd have had to irrigate the bone.

— You'd have to what?

— Irrigate the bone.

Then, as if he'd just thought of something obscene, the doctor blushed slightly and went away.

I learned a new phrase on the second day Julius was in hospital. It was 'Index of Anxiety'. When he was admitted, Julius's position on the Index of Anxiety had been very high. Then the antibiotics went to work and Julius began to move down the Index. Few cases stay that high up the Index of Anxiety for long. They'll go one way or the other. There was one baby, though, in the middle of the ward. He was in the ordinary sort of new-born cot, he was very small and he was swaddled in white, and the noise he made filled the ward even though it wasn't very loud. It was a kind of lonely kittenish crying broken by little catches in the throat. The baby's parents were usually there, sitting against the wall, and sometimes they were crying and sometimes they just sat looking utterly forlorn beside huddles of relations.

I asked a nurse about the baby.

— How old is he. A week?

— Three months actually. It's a classic Fail-to-Thrive.

The next day the 'Fail-to-Thrive' was transferred to another hospital. His position on the Index of Anxiety had risen, probably fatally, higher. The parents sat, tearless, unmoving, as nurses chattily performed efficient actions with drip tubes and trolleys. And milling around were some melancholy older children waiting for surgery for a condition which this hospital specialized in treating, a genetic disorder that transforms the nose, making it into something like a cartoon witch's – while the Fail-to-Thrive was wheeled away, the nose children sadly toured the ward on tatty toy cars.

Susan, my wife, stayed at night with Julius in the hospital. I was there throughout the days but by night time I would nervily become more of a liability than a help. Alone in the house, sleepless, I would go up to Julius's room. Seashell aeroplane mobile hanging from the ceiling. Brightly coloured poster of farm animals. The Ernest Hemingway Adventure Map of the World, which someone had once given to me and which I had deferred on to my son. I'd been struck one night, in this room, watching Julius sleep, by the realization that my love for this boy was boundless, I couldn't imagine its limits; this was still a relatively new emotion for me, and now the hospital experience was mixed up with it in an awful way. I played with Julius's cars and remembered him rolling them back to me. It was as if I were in the first stages of trying to invent a preferable universe. And when I caught a reflection of myself, my mirror face was almost unrecognizable. It looked like somebody else and it took a while to work out who, and then I recognized the expression: I'd seen it on the face of a father in New York about ten years before.

After I moved to New York from London my first job was at a video rental store on the Upper East Side. The most annoying employee there was a rich boy called Greg. Greg was finishing his summer job before he went on to college. He was a few years younger than the rest of us there and he kept trying to make us be his friends. He kept importuning us to go to 'the apartment' with him; we would have fun at 'the apartment'; there would be drugs there. It got so that eventually it was easier to give in than continue to resist, so one night Vinny and Tom and Neil and I went back with Greg after work.

On the walk over Greg seemed nervous. Usually Greg was over-talkative, trying to brag his way into our respect. On the walk over to the apartment Greg was silent. He held a set of keys in his hand and played with them as if they were worry beads.

— Is this your apartment? asked Neil.

— Kinda, said Greg.

— What do you mean, kinda? said Tom.

— Just kinda, said Greg.

The apartment was in an old handsome building on Park Avenue. The doorman nodded us through and we took the elevator up to the fourth floor. Greg fumbled with the keys and finally got one to work and led us into a plushly moneyed place that was enormous for Manhattan (we all lived in small cockroached spaces). We'd been laughing about something but fell silent when we saw the man in the living room armchair. This was not Greg's father; we had met Greg's father a couple of times, in the video store. Greg's father looked exactly like Greg, just older and more complete. This man looked nothing like Greg. He wore expensive trousers and a silk shirt open at the throat, and expensive socks that were so thin they were almost transparent. He looked up from the book he was reading in the armchair. Tom and I hid the cigarettes we were smoking behind our backs.

— Great to see you! How you doing, Greg? Come in, boys. Great to see you!

— How you doing? said Greg. His voice sounded proud and smug.

— You boys go right on in. You want beers?

We shook our heads.

— Beers would be good, said Greg.

— Go right on in. I'll get the beers.

The man laid down his book, pushed back his grey hair and, smiling, leapt out of his chair like a boy.

Greg led us round a corridor corner and unlocked a door at the end.

— That was Johnny's dad, said Greg. This is Johnny's room.

Johnny's room had movie starlet posters on the wall and pictures of rock bands and a lot of pricey technology dustless in every corner. Johnny's room was large. It had a queen-sized double bed and above it the only bookshelf which held Johnny's stack of sword & sorcery and war books. In the middle of the room stood a large glass-topped desk. Johnny's room was airless and it had that smell of absence, of lack of use and life.

Greg sat down at the desk. Vinny and Neil and I sat on the bed. Tom strolled around the room, picking things up and putting them down again.

— Where's Johnny? asked Vinny.

Greg pulled open a drawer and, without looking up, tossed a bag of marijuana towards Tom.

— Roll us some joints, Tom.

From the same drawer came a pile of cocaine which Greg poured on to the glass top of the desk. He set to work with a gold AmEx card to cut it into lines. There was a knock on the door. Tom covered over the marijuana with a magazine. Greg carried on cutting the coke. The man from the living room came in with six beers on a tray. He laid the tray down on the floor. There was a scared happy smile on his face.

— Beers! I'll be in the living room. Call if you want anything.

— Sure thing, said Greg.

We drank beer and smoked marijuana and snorted cocaine. None of us especially cared for cocaine, but we were all young and poor enough to enjoy consuming expensive drugs for free. Greg tried to get conversations going but they all just drifted away and popped. We were all feeling uncomfortable and we weren't sure why. Tom asked again where Johnny was, and Vinny wanted to know about the guy with the hair and the socks, but Greg ignored the questions. He showed us books and magazines and he played some music on the stereo, and he removed the dust sheet from the computer and loaded it up with some of the latest games that none of us was interested to play. Vinny stretched and yawned. Tom started to say that his girlfriend would be wondering where he was. Neil had his eyes closed and might have been asleep. So, in desperation, to keep us there, Greg told us the story of Johnny and their friendship and his stupid death.

Johnny was killed by accident. He had been in a video game parlour on Broadway and 45th Street playing a kung fu game with Greg standing beside him. Johnny and Greg had been friends since they were small. They'd been sent to the same private schools. Their parents had got divorced at around the same time. They had smoked their first joint together and snorted their first lines of cocaine together, and, at the same expensive summer camp, got laid together.

One night, an ordinary night, Greg went round to Johnny's room. Their nights always began in Johnny's room. Sometimes just Johnny and Greg together, and sometimes a whole gang of them in there, making teenage noise, doing rich-boy teenage things. Since the divorce of his parents Johnny lived with his father. That night, Greg was let in by Johnny's father, Italian suit trousers, silk shirt open at the throat, feet in transparent socks, long slicked-back greying hair. Johnny's father was making his own preparations for the night and didn't bother Greg with conversation. Greg went into Johnny's room. Johnny was lying on the bed playing air guitar to a Led Zeppelin song. Johnny was a handsome boy. He was tall and muscular. His own hair was black and styled a lot like his father's. He used the same mousse spray to sweep it back and hold it there. In his left ear lobe he wore a *diamanté* stud. Johnny was Jewish – or at least his parents were – but to Jewish eyes he looked Italian. (To Italian eyes he looked maybe Puerto Rican. And to Puerto Ricans he was obviously Jewish.) Girls always went for Johnny. This didn't make Greg jealous. Greg accepted that his friend was handsomer and cleverer and more attractive than him. In Johnny's company Greg felt more than himself.

They got through a couple of joints and a few lines of cocaine. Then they went out, in Johnny's father's sports car, stopping off at their favourite video game parlour. The parlour was called World of Fun and they had been coming here ever since they were about ten. They always had a favourite game at World of Fun and this season it was a kung fu fighting game at which they were evenly matched. They went in, changed five dollars into quarters and waited their turn at the kung fu fighting machine.

And in came Johnny's destroyer. Johnny's destroyer had just got out of prison where he had served a sentence for aggravated assault. Johnny's destroyer had a weaselly sidekick with him and a baseball bat in his hands. Before being sent to jail Johnny's destroyer had been promised by his girlfriend that she would wait for him. While he was in jail friends had reported on her infidelity. And now the destroyer was out; he hadn't decided yet how to deal with the woman but, on his second day of freedom, he was looking to deliver retribution to the man who had cuckolded him. A description had been given. The cuckolder wore a diamond stud in his left ear. He was Puerto Rican. His hair was black and swept back. He hung out in World of Fun. He always wore a leather jacket.

Johnny often wore a leather jacket. He was wearing it that night. Johnny was not the cuckolder. He had never met the ex-prisoner nor the straying girlfriend. Johnny was about to be fatally unlucky. The place at the machine came free. Greg stepped aside for Johnny to take it. Johnny slotted in a dollar's worth of quarters. He selected two-player operation. He entered their initials. He opened his legs farther apart, rolled his head like Mike Tyson, tested the action on the joystick and started to play.

And the next moment the destroyer walked around the aisle of machines – the sidekick shrilly pointed out Johnny – Greg looked around to check out the commotion – the destroyer stepped forward, muttered something like, '*This is for Ramona!*' and lifted his baseball bat with both hands and brought it down on the top of Johnny's head. As Johnny was falling, he was hit twice more, on the back of the head. Then the destroyer and the weasel left the scene, and Greg's best friend was on the floor, gushing blood from a smashed, dead skull.

After the funeral, as they were walking slowly away, Johnny's father gave a set of keys to Greg.

— This one's for the door of the building, and this one's for the apartment, and the long one, that's for Johnny's room.

— Yes, said Greg. I recognize it.

— I want you to use the place just like you always did. You guys had a lot of fun, didn't you? Bring your pals.

— Thank you, said Greg, because he couldn't think of anything else to say.

— And the car, too. Whenever you feel like it, I want you to know, just ask for the keys. I don't have another set so I can't give it you but just ask. Any time.

— Thank you, said Greg.

The first time Greg returned to Johnny's room, he went there by himself. He let himself in with the key that Johnny's father had given him. Johnny's father was sitting in the living room watching something on the TV. His hair had turned entirely grey and it was uncombed and swept back. There were no sounds coming from Johnny's room, otherwise things were as they used to be.

— How you doing, Greg? asked Johnny's father.

— How you doing? said Greg.

He paused there a moment, waiting to see if there was going to be anything more to say but Johnny's father had turned his attention back to the TV, so Greg just went on, down the corridor, past the bathroom, into Johnny's room.

Johnny's room was almost exactly as it used to be, maybe a little cleaner. The stereo was switched on. The TV showed its little red sleep-mode light. The records and CDs were tidily scattered as if someone had just been choosing what to play. The girlie mags were where they used to be, behind the war books. Greg sat on the bed, then that made him nervous so he went to the glass-topped desk instead. There was a poem under the glass, typewritten or maybe computer printed. It was called 'How Do I Describe My Son?' And it was a horrible poem, full of snapshot memories of childhood and its little landmarks – bicycle rides, the tooth fairy, first tuft of underarm hair. Greg opened the drawer. There was a neat package of marijuana in there he didn't remember from the last time. He chose a magazine and laid it over the poem. He rolled a joint and started to smoke it while he browsed through the pictures trying to imagine which Johnny's favourite girls would be. Then came a knock on the door and before Greg could take evasive action, the door was open and Johnny's father was standing there and Greg held the lighted joint under the desk and kept the smoke in his mouth and he could feel himself ready to choke.

— How you doing? said Johnny's father.

Greg nodded, couldn't hold on to the smoke any longer and let it all billow out.

— How you doing? he said.

— Got everything you need?

— Sure do.

— Sorry to disturb you, just wanted to say I'm going out now but if you're hungry you just help yourself to whatever's in the refrigerator. You want a beer, maybe?

— No thanks. I'm OK for beer.

— Greg?

— …?

— I'm glad to see you. I mean that. Next time, you might want to bring some friends along? Make a party of it.

— I will. I promise.

— I'll say so long, then.

— So long.

Johnny's father shut the door quietly behind him.

Greg finished the story about Johnny's stupid death and its aftermath. He leaned forward,

— And there's always coke and grass in the drawer!

I said I was going to use the bathroom. I had to pass through the living room to get to it. Johnny's father was in the armchair, limbs stretched out; he was holding a book and staring at it. Through the window a bridge was visible and the lighted windows of apartment blocks. I sat down, on a companion armchair. Johnny's father looked up from his book, he nodded at me and I nodded back and then he turned his attention back to his book again. We sat there like that for a while.

From time to time noises rose up out of Johnny's room. Led Zeppelin. Black Sabbath. The Clash. Tom's voice was getting louder, more belligerent. Vinny was faking someone else's voice and making Neil laugh. Every now and again Johnny's father would look up and smile. I'd smile back. The room got darker.

— Kids, said Johnny's father abruptly, not looking up.

— Excuse me?

— People say the time goes by so quick, he said.

— I bet it does.

— I'm thinking of redecorating Johnny's room. It's beginning to look kind of dated. You know what I mean?

He smiled at me. He looked very pleased with himself and very, very sad. The smile faded away. What was left was an expression I'd never seen before and wasn't going to see for another ten years until I caught sight of my reflection alone in Julius's room.

He waited for me to say something.

— Everything in Johnny's room is very new, I said.

— You noticed that? That's not so good. You shouldn't notice it. It's just that I want to keep everything up to date. I want to keep it as he would like it, you know?

He looked at me sharply. As if I was to blame for something. Then he looked down at his book again.

— You guys have everything you need?

— Yes, I said.

— You can borrow the car if you like.

— Thank you, I said. I don't think it'll be necessary.

We sat in more silence for a while, and then I went back into Johnny's room. Tom was on the phone to his girlfriend. Vinny was telling Greg about when he was twelve and had run away from home to join the circus. Neil had fallen asleep on the floor. Greg was at the desk looking at the other people in the room, part-pleased because he was doing his duty by his dead friend and part-distraught because things weren't at all how they were meant to be.

It is impossible I suppose, in this culture, to recover from the death of a child. The death of your parents is part of the natural order, but the death of your children must feel like a violation of it. (Although maybe it is different in other places and times where the infant mortality rate is much higher and families correspondingly larger.) I never went back to Johnny's room. It was too creepy. The only similar room I'd ever been in was when I was sixteen and I went with some schoolfriends to a rock star's parents' house. They'd kept the rock star's bedroom exactly as it had been the day he left it, twelve years before. As if, just like in Johnny's room, he might be about to return any moment, and would want to see his Bob Dylan posters on the walls hanging off at the same sellotape tilt as when he'd left.

Having children forces upon you a different relationship with memory and time. As you watch your child grow, each stage of development feels absolute, sucks time into itself. He can focus his eyes now. He makes these little cooing noises. The previous stage is almost forgotten. And then comes along a different time. A new perpetual present. He's lying in an iron hospital bed that's much too big for him. He has a drip tube tapped into the side of his foot. He sleeps more than he ever used to. He's sick. And he doesn't make those cooing noises any more and you can hardly remember them. This, as Johnny's father had learned or was trying to make himself learn, is the problem. Memory. Fix memory and maybe time will look after itself.

The antibiotics did their job with Julius. The swelling of the mastoid bone went down; the infection did not spread and develop into meningitis as the doctors had privately worried it would; he was soon healthy and home again. But each night he was in hospital I sat in his room for a while. I made his mobile move as if a baby's hand had just touched it. I flicked through his picture books. I inspected the Ernest Hemingway Adventure Map of the World as if I were holding my son up to look at it for us to plan imaginary journeys together. I caught a glimpse of what it is like to lose a child and find your only way to deal with it is to pretend.

Mike Phillips

Mike Phillips was born in Guyana, and
then went to school and grew up in
London. After pursuing several different
ways of making a living, among them
teaching, journalism, broadcasting and
lecturing, he became a full-time
novelist. Along with various other work,
he has published five novels, the most
recent being *The Dancing Face* (Harper-
Collins, May 1997). Under his pseudonym,
Joe Canzius, he has published two
thrillers, *Fast Road to Nowhere* (Vista,
October 1996), and *Dead Men Also
Dream* (Vista, April 1997). Mike Phillips is
currently Writer in Residence at the South
Bank Centre, Royal Festival Hall, London.

The Second Coming

Mike Phillips gives a
repeat performance

My first child was born on a bright sunny morning in October 1974. I'd spent the previous twenty-four hours sitting in a waiting room at University College Hospital, so I'd had plenty of time to think. At about eleven o'clock a nurse came in and told me that I had a son, and I rushed down the corridor, wanting to run, my only thought to see him. They were wheeling him out of the room in a cot, and I walked alongside, taking my first good look. He seemed impossibly little, battered and exhausted, a fighter at the end of a long struggle, his face bruised and marked by the forceps they'd used. We came to a door, and someone was trying to hurry me, pushing me out of the way, but I held on to the edge of the cot, and stopped it going through for a moment. In that moment he opened his eyes and looked at me.

I remember that look even now. Dead level, something speculative about it, wondering. I've seen it many times since then, when he wants to tell me about something that's upset him, or when we're talking seriously and I've said something that puzzles or annoys him. It's a serious look which seems to come from the eyes I first saw so many years ago, when that straightforward questing stare was all there was to him, asking the same question – so who's this guy?

A few minutes later I went out into the autumn sunshine, moving like a sleepwalker, automatically. I felt as if I was there and not there all at the same time, as if the pavement, the buildings, the glitter of the sun on a windscreen were products of my mind, insubstantial, unreal, and for the moment, I couldn't figure out whether I was in the grip of some trauma brought on by the experience or whether I was just simply knackered.

I went round the corner to a café in Tottenham Court Road and bought a ham sandwich. I hadn't eaten since the previous morning and now I was starving. Walking back to the hospital I worried about the fact that, even though I'd been turning things over in my mind for the last couple of days, I hadn't come to any conclusions or made any decisions about what would happen or how we would live. At the time we lived in a bedsitter in north London. I didn't have a job and there was nothing in sight. Freelancing and doing odd jobs brought in barely enough to pay the rent. From time to time during that morning I felt like a man setting out in a leaky rowboat to cross the Atlantic.

I can remember now that look my son gave me, but I can't remember thinking clearly about anything else during that period. What sticks in my mind is the fact that I had some idea of writing a diary about our life together, which just goes to show you what my mood was like – a kaleidoscope in which numbness gave way to fear which gave way to a crazy sentimentality.

Back in the waiting room I sat down and tried to begin writing my thoughts of the previous two days, but as soon as I opened the notebook I realized that all I could recall was a jumble of memories and impressions. Struggling desperately to get a fix on my feelings I began scribbling a few sentences. *My son was born this morning*, I wrote. *He opened his eyes and looked at me. Now I know what love is.*

After that I closed the book, and I never wrote anything else in it. It's still in my possession, and occasionally, tidying up, I run across it, the covers neat and clean, three sentences stark against the empty pages.

There was never any question in my mind at any time during my life about whether or not I was going to be a father. I knew it was going to happen. I knew, also, that it was something to do with the logic of being a man. In the culture of the place and time where I was born 'father' was a simple biological description. I knew kids whose fathers denied their existence. I knew kids whose fathers hardly spoke except when they hit them. I knew kids who had not seen their fathers for years. Later on I knew men whose adolescence had been spent in a battle of wills with their fathers. But, at the time, none of this made a dent in the concept of the thing. If you were lucky, your father looked after you with kindness and concern. But even if he was a bad father, no one else would do. The notion of 'fathering' was beside the point. In those circumstances contemporary buzzwords like 'nurture' and 'caring' were unknown, and, if they had been, would have made no sense. A father was the man whose potency had charged you with the spark of life, and so fatherhood and manhood were inextricably linked.

There was something about the very word that was electric, mystical, redolent of sacral power – God the Father. Fathers had the power to bless, the strength to protect and when you got right down to the wire, they could condemn, punish, cast you into the outer darkness. The Church certainly knew what it was doing when it gave its priests the title 'Father'.

I had precisely this sense of awe about my own father while he was alive, and my first clear memory of him contains a blend of worship, fear, shame and guilt which brings him back to me immediately, sharp and clearly present, the way I encounter him in my dreams. On this occasion I was still very young, about three years old, I suppose, and I was playing about in a pile of junk under our house, when I heard my father shouting my name. I was crouching out of sight inside an old cupboard and instead of answering I stayed hidden. Looking back, I don't know why I didn't answer right away. I suppose it must have been a combination of fear and mischief, but the longer he called, his voice sounding louder and more furious, the more difficult it became to come out of hiding. Even when the rest of the family joined in, a chorus of voices, I still didn't move. After a while they seemed to give up looking for me and things went quiet, so I crawled out to take a look. Everyone was clustered round the gate and I was just in time to see my father, dressed in his soldier's uniform, standing in the back of a lorry which was speeding off down the road. I understood immediately. While I'd been hiding from him, he'd been calling me to say goodbye. I started then, to run after the lorry, to try to catch him to say I was sorry, but it was too late. He didn't come back for a long time.

He died in the year my first son was born. I still dream about him, a tall young man, younger than I am now, and I watch him cautiously, wondering what he thinks about me, wanting to tell him many things. One time I rang my mum to tell her, and she said, 'He's trying to tell you something.' 'Well, I'd figured that much out for myself,' I told her. 'I just wish I knew what he was trying to say.'

Sometimes I get a message from him, through the medium of my own feelings, a faint echo, which is a blend of memory and emotion. During our first years in England the cinema was my passion. I was only one of two black boys at my school, and it was a long time before I found a circle of friends. Sitting alone in the dark absorbed by the hypnotic flicker of the screen seemed natural and inevitable. Sometimes I'd sit there until they played the national anthem, nerving myself up for the dash home, because late at night the streets of Hackney were still dangerous territory for a black teenager. At the top of our road I'd see my dad standing under a lamp post. When he saw me coming he'd turn and go back in the house. In my head I still carry this image of him, standing up straight, steady as a rock in that circle of smoky light, peering through the darkness, trying to catch a glimpse of me.

When my first son was only a baby, a perfect little man, lying still and beautiful in his cot, I would have a recurring nightmare. We'd be out somewhere, and I'd turn around and find him gone, or suddenly I'd be miles away from where I'd left the pram, or I'd be holding him, running the gauntlet of angry crowds, faces contorted, hands and weapons lashing out at him. Waking up, I would go to take a look in his room, make sure he was all right. Sometimes, in the early hours of the morning, I'd be sitting at my desk, writing, trying to find the right words, and I'd hear a sound behind me. When I turned round he'd be there, gazing at me, clutching his little blue blanket to his chest.

What I didn't know then, in the middle of my anxiety, was that this would be the easiest bit. Some varieties of parenting are easier, less complicated, than others, and there are special difficulties about being a black father in a society like ours. Take these pointers, for instance. In my son's run-up to the GCSE exams I attended the year's first open day where one of the teachers we encountered was a well-intentioned young man, who gave me a brief and well-rehearsed lecture about the importance of having books in the home and encouraging my son to read. By this time I was a university lecturer, a published author and my own teaching career must have begun while the teacher in front of me was still in the cradle. My son had been playing with books before he could walk, and reading before he went near a school. But this particular teacher had no way of knowing this, and, I suppose, he had no way of knowing how patronizing his remarks were. What he saw in front of him was a black man, and that gave him his cue.

Another time, about nine in the morning, my son had just set out on some errand, when I heard the doorbell ring. Thinking he'd forgotten his keys I opened it, to see him standing beside a policeman who had stopped him a few feet away from the front door and insisted on checking that he lived in the house from which he'd just emerged. This was Holland Park, but the policeman, new on the beat, was barely polite, and once I'd reassured him about my son he turned his attention to me. 'How long have you been living here, sir?' was his next question.

In normal circumstances families have a sort of contract with the society in which they exist. The bargain is that you protect your children, and induct them into the conventions which govern our lives. In return you get an assurance of safety, and the promise of access to a range of services and opportunities. In practice life is unpredictable, because that's how things are, but, small print aside, most parents believe in this guarantee. Generally, fathers inherit a sense that they have a crucial public role to play in this process, which is precisely the background of feeling that gives a sharp edge to some of the current debates about parenting.

In recent years white men have begun to express their uneasiness about the undermining and erosion of their public status. By contrast, black men in our society have had to live with a continuing sense of being under attack. All of us have our prospects determined or limited by discrimination. Catch 22. Keep your head down, stay out of trouble and soldier through the routine of giving your family some sort of security, and you get typecast as a passive object of attitudes and conditions against which any man of spirit would rebel. If you take chances, pursue your ambitions and then fail, it qualifies you as an exemplar of the irresponsibility and inadequacy of your generation of black fathers. You can't win, because, either way, the problems your children encounter will sooner or later be laid at your door by a slew of experts and gurus in the classroom, or on TV, radio, in newspapers and through every other medium available.

Shortly after my first son was born I began to experience new and curious feelings. I don't mean the sort of sentiment you feel sitting and holding your child, poring over the sheer marvel of having produced this tiny, perfect creature. I expected that. This was something different, a cultural thing, I would have to call it, and the unexpected quality of my emotion was probably due to the way that I'd begun to think about 'culture'. This was different to the ideas about culture with which I'd grown up. As a young immigrant I understood that we, that is, people from the country where I was born, were marked out and linked together by our customs: our food, our music, the dialect we spoke. We were accustomed to the idea that people from our region had always travelled far afield in search of work and better prospects. Sometimes they came back with the strangest customs and habits, but that made no difference, because you could live at the North Pole and eat whale meat, or wear a grass skirt or learn to speak Chinese, without ceasing to be one of us. Such things were only the décor of one's life. The culture was what we were inside, the way we felt about each other and about the world.

A couple of decades later, by the time my son was born, the culture to which I was supposed to belong had become 'black culture', and every time you heard the word it meant someone was trying to sell you something – a record, a ticket, membership of some group or allegiance to some campaign they had going. 'Our culture' was the phrase used by the dickhead who argued that I ought to plait my son's hair in dreadlocks, even though I had grown up having my head scraped to the scalp every fortnight under a mango tree, my father watching the barber sternly. 'Cut it clean,' he'd go. 'Your culture' was the phrase the teacher uttered when she read a poem written in the Barbadian dialect to my son's class, using what she imagined was a Jamaican accent, never knowing the difference altered the feel and the meaning of it. 'Culture' was what the man said down the market, when he tugged on my arm and tried to sell me fake African carvings or a tie-dye Rasta T-shirt or a full colour photo of a ripe ackee. In the environment we live in, 'our culture' has become a sort of mental junk food.

The culture I had actually been part of had no status in this marketplace. It wasn't even available any more outside of a collective memory, which was rapidly fading as previous generations disappeared. What hit me, though, with an unexpected force and clarity, was that I'd grown up believing, and I still believed, that being a father was like being a link in a chain. My job was to pass on to my son the feelings and emotions which had come down through my own father, the same collective memory which was part of what I was. Suddenly, the memory of my own childhood, its sights and sounds and smells and emotions had taken on a new reality, as if time had folded in on itself. Suddenly, I had this desperate longing for my son to share those things. Long-forgotten and disparate scraps of experience kept on floating to the surface. Chasing rats through the yard, sucking on the sweet pulp of a mango till the juice ran down my chin, watching a flock of vultures climbing into the sky, waking up to the insistent beat of the surf crashing on to the shore.

What made these images so painful was the fact that they belonged to a life which had vanished and which my son could never now enter or even understand. In my own life I had the sense that when I looked back past my father I could see versions of him stretching far into the landscape, at least to slavery. By contrast I had come together with my son on the other side of a break from my old world, which had disjointed memory and cut me off from the springs of feeling that flowed from the past. I had the sense that when he looked past me what he saw would be obscure, a vacuum, perhaps, which could only be filled by a constructed 'culture' faked up from the fantasies sketched out by entrepreneurs and politicians. This was it, I realized, as I sat holding him, early Sunday mornings in front of the telly, watching the *Mister Men*. There was a hole in my soul, a cultural thing.

I have three sisters and two brothers. For me this was part of the natural order, and after I separated from my son's mum I knew I'd always feel a sense of regret and guilt, because we'd never given him the flock of siblings he deserved. Not that he seemed to mind, and he always said he didn't when I asked him about it. On the other hand, when I thought about having another child I thought about him first, how he would feel, and somehow the thought made me defensive on his behalf; I kept asking myself how he would feel. Opportunities came and went. I felt no urgency or any great desire for more children. One is enough, I thought. My mother raised the subject whenever I saw her. She now lived in the USA, so that wasn't often. 'You're not getting any younger,' she'd say.

This wasn't an idea which caused me any great worry. Something else happened round about the time that my big son, as I now call him, had finished taking his A Levels. For a couple of years I'd been settled into a relationship which made me happy. Conversations about babies followed discussions about the biological clock. Decisions were called for. I was kind of neutral about the prospect, until I caught myself, at odd times, thinking about what it had felt like when my big son was still a baby. All at once I could remember bits of the life we'd shared as if it had been the day before. Lying in bed, asleep, next to his mum, I'd wake up with a start as he crawled over me to squeeze himself into the middle, between us, his sharp little elbows jabbing a space clear. When he got his first trike, a wooden thing with red plastic wheels, he'd run it across the floor and smash it into the wall, repeatedly, laughing like a maniac. When I played my Big Youth album on the record player he'd run to the sofa, jump up and begin bouncing excitedly. Suddenly, I missed him, although I saw him practically every day, as if he'd grown up and gone away already. I still loved him with all the passion I had ever felt, but this was different. I wanted my little baby back.

I told him about it one morning, as we drove up the A1, on the way north to see some relatives. He gave me a smile of adult tolerance. 'I wondered about that,' he said. 'I thought maybe you never had any more children because of me. It was an extreme sacrifice, though. I wouldn't have minded.'

I was flabbergasted. I'm not sure why. Maybe because I'd spent so much time worrying about it. 'What about now?' I asked him. He thought for a bit. 'It's OK,' he said. 'Be good to have a little brother.'

Over the next few days I felt a weird kind of peace, as if all the elements of my life were at last beginning to jell. 'Let's do it,' I told her.

During the pregnancy he came to live with us. At night I'd go round locking the windows, and look in on him as he lay in bed reading, then I'd climb the stairs. Sometimes I felt like the king of the castle, everything I cared about most under one roof. By then we knew he'd be going away to university in a few months. It will all be different this time next year, I kept thinking, and I'd feel a thrill of something like fear.

My little son, the baby, was born at UCH, same as his brother. I was particular about that. While my partner sweated through the labour, my big son and I were together all night, sometimes sitting next to her, sometimes standing in the corridor, sometimes pacing down Tottenham Court Road. We talked about football, about what it would be like at university, about my father and what it had been like when I left school. The night wore on and I felt more and more pleased and grateful for his presence. I needed him then, the first time I'd needed him in that way, and he was great, a real support, like one of my brothers would have been.

When the baby arrived the first thing I noticed was that he was bruised and battered, a little fighter at the end of a long struggle. Then he opened his eyes and looked at me. How strong the resemblance to his big brother was, both reassuring and confusing at the same time.

Holding the little one I kept thinking about how I'd held the big one all those years ago. Now he was taller than me, he could run faster and beat me at arm-wrestling, into the bargain. In my mind there was a circle of forces continually pulling in different directions.

But a lot had changed. In the last nineteen years I had learned to be a father. The pangs and pains and agonies of uncertainty I had felt the first time round had simply vanished. Most of this was about familiarity with what would happen. I knew all about mixed feeding and burping, no problem. I could bring up a kid. I knew that now. The other thing I was about to learn was more complicated. Being a father never ends. When the baby was a few months old I drove my son up to the university for his first day. Registration, carrying his luggage to his room, looking around. Driving away, his mum cried. Everything and nothing had changed. He wasn't a baby any more, except in some private space of our memory.

Back home I hugged the little one. Before I had him, when I was thinking about it, I'd had a secret fear that my love would be like a cake to be divided between the two children. No such thing. Whatever it was had doubled, simply multiplied by two. The other odd thing was that I'd imagined that being with the baby would wipe out my feelings of nostalgia and loss. Instead, there they were, faded a little, but still, on occasion, as strong and painful as ever.

Entering his final year at university, my big son told me he was applying for a postgraduate course in Madrid. 'I want to be away for a while,' he said. 'Stand on my own two feet, away from you and my mum. Find myself.'

I told him it was a great idea. Later on the baby and I watched him drive away down the road, little brother crowing 'bye bye'. 'In another eighteen years,' I told him, 'that will be you.' Then I caught myself thinking that while it was possible that I might have eighteen years left, it was unlikely that I would be around to watch him go and leave me behind, the world all new in his eyes, fresh youth on the brink of adventure. That's the one drawback about the baby. Twenty years ago, when I started this journey, the horizon had no limits. Now I know what I only suspected back then. One day I'll die. With any luck I'll have another twenty years, maybe it will be tomorrow. All that I'll leave is a memory. They'll bring it out and dust it off sometimes. They'll tell their kids about me, and they'll say, 'That was my father.' That's more than a hope. I know that's how it will be. Being a father never ends.

Neil Spencer

Journalist and writer Neil
Spencer works for the
Observer, for whom he covers
music, astrology and popular
culture. Formerly editor of *New
Musical Express* during *NME*'s
most infamous and successful
years, he has also worked for
Arena, *20/20*, *Elle* and
numerous other magazines.
Happily harassed by his three
children, he is currently writing
a children's book.

Daddy Cool

Neil Spencer on why you'll
never be as hip as your
kids

It must be great to grow up with a cool dad,' mused a bachelor
friend round the pub table, after he'd enquired after the welfare of
my three children.

'How do you mean?' I asked.

'Well, my dad rode to work on a bike dressed in a horrible old
mac,' he went on. 'He was nice, but he was just an ordinary straight
bloke, he didn't know anything about music or clothes or stuff like
that. He wasn't hip, he was just a bloke, know what I mean?'

I knew what he meant. And I have to admit that, whatever else I
pass on to my children, I take a foolish pride in knowing that they'll
inherit a cracking library of first-edition hardbacks (review copies,
mostly) and dog-eared paperbacks, along with an irresponsibly large
record collection of prime twentieth-century music and some tasty
Susie Cooper plates gleaned from various flea markets. My son
might even find a few vintage ties and suits worth adding to his
wardrobe. But cool? It's hard to inherit cool and an illusion to think
you can bequeath it. Kids don't want cool – it's stuck down their
infant craws every time they turn on the telly, mope along the high
street or bustle round the playground. What kids want is a dad. And
dads, by definition, are not cool.

In the old days – let's say anything pre-Beatles – dads were never expected to be cool. Knobbly of physiognomy, variously remote, surly and indulgent of mood, dads inhabited a world where the trivia of teendom didn't impinge. They were there to infuriate you with their scoffing remarks on your favourite pop stars, to insist, 'You're never going out dressed like that,' when you donned your must-wear Saturday-night duds (which you then changed into out of sight of the house), and generally to reassure you that the grown-up world was deadly boring and that you would never grow up to be like that.

In other words, fathers supplied what poet and writer Robert Bly has called 'the oedipal wall', an authority figure voicing those inescapable demands for mature behaviour that suddenly rear up around puberty and against which any self-respecting son (and, in a different way, daughter) will rightly rebel.

The kind of authority fathers supplied in the old patriarchal order ranged from kindly concern to downright brutality. The Victorian legacy was that fathers govern their families with the avenging hand of Jehovah. In practice this often meant that fathers became little more than legally sanctioned bullies, with the fight between them and their children, particularly their sons, conducted in a mood of vindictiveness where physical violence was never far away.

Underlying the obstinacy and rage of the fathers of the old order was the conviction that they knew best, that they were what they were and that no son or daughter of theirs was going to turn out differently. It was an attitude that cut across class barriers. The image, familiar from kitchen-sink films like *Billy Liar*, of the dour working-class father forbidding his son to bother with 'all that education nonsense' and 'filling up your head with airy-fairy ideas about being an artist' is now cultural cliché. Scenes of middle-class parents' incomprehension at their children's desire to turn down the pinstripe suit and a steady job in the family firm for a life of idealistic, long-haired bohemia are not far behind.

This was the world of the 'generation gap', of parents and children staring at each other from opposite sides of a divide defined by the advent of mass-technology, consumerdom and cultural upsurge. Drug experiences were another vital part of the shift from deference to disrespect, sexual repression to sexual experimentation, 'straight' culture to 'youth' culture. Not all fathers in the old patriarchy were harsh and unsympathetic – many were kind and attentive – but even the best of them couldn't help but be distant from the vastly different experiences of their children. Having grown up with deprivation, hardship and the trauma of war, they had struggled to ensure their kids didn't endure the same. Their incomprehension at the attitudes of the generation that followed deserves as much sympathy as contempt. Bob Dylan, among the first to declare that sons and daughters were beyond the command of their parents, also showed empathy with the older generation a few years later. In 'Tears of Rage' he took the voice of a parent baffled at being thrown aside and 'put away'.

Conventional wisdom held that the sixties generation would eventually find its come-uppance on the receiving end of the next generation gap, an idea confirmed in minor key when the punk insurrection of the late seventies cocked its safety-pinned snook as much at hippiedom as at the status quo of queen and government; there was to be 'no future' for anyone. But punks, too, have now become parents, and while the advent of rave culture has drawn a distinctive generational barrier of sorts – 'At least in my day the music wasn't made by sodding computers,' goes the grumble – the generation gap of the nineties is nothing like its sixties equivalent. Dads, too, like Oasis and Blur, know what dropping a tab of acid feels like and can't help but maintain a lively interest in the progress of youth cults which often worship at the shrine of the sixties.

In this new landscape, the danger is not that parents won't understand their children, but that they'll be actively competing with them, a scenario brilliantly satirized by *Absolutely Fabulous*, in which a trendy mum is the despair of her level-headed daughter. Today, the generation gap is being squeezed from both sides, with kids accelerated into premature adolescence and parents determined to stay 'forever young'. Ten-year-olds are courted by an avaricious free market eager to instil awareness of which logo they should have on their trainers, and early teenagers are increasingly likely to be fooling around with booze and drugs, the 'alco-pop' boom being an ugly illustration of brewers' determination to get their customers hooked early. Forget that rosy scenario where a proud father buys his son his first pint; long before the legal drinking age today's kids are likely to have tippled more than their share of 5 per cent proof lemonade.

Where fathers fit into this new picture is a question made more vexed by the wider crisis surrounding parenthood and fatherhood in particular. The components of the crisis are many. Some are economic in origin. In the post-industrialized global economy, the old idea of the male breadwinner is no longer tenable. Women, too, now demand jobs and careers and seem more able to fit in with the kind of casual work on offer. It isn't only the muscle-bound blue-collar male who has been hit by this change; if middle-class women want a career, either their men have to look after the kids or the children get raised by an assortment of child-minders, au pairs, nursery teachers and nannies, while their parents vanish for most of the week to pay for all this child care.

Feminist attacks on the patriarchal order have also found their mark. Remote and absent fathers have been rightfully admonished under this barrage, but it has also helped to undermine the very idea of fatherhood itself. Tony Blair, expressing the opinion that two parents are better than one, found himself under furious attack from left-wing feminists for whom fathers have become not just expendable but intrinsically evil; aren't children better off without their nasty, phallocentric aggression? (I have seen several feminist mothers react with horror when they see their two-year-old sons seize coat-hangers and sticks as stand-ins for the toy guns and swords banned from the household as non-PC items. 'My God,' goes the realization, 'it isn't just nurture, after all – this stuff is in them from the start!' To which we have to plead guilty, while pointing out that wanting a gun at three – preferably an inter-galactic laser with sound effects – is perfectly OK. It's when you still want one at twenty-three that it becomes a problem.)

For those of us determined to be neither absent nor remote from our children, the question of how we behave as fathers remains confusingly open. The old patriarchal template is clearly not an option, and most of us couldn't revert to playing the heavy-handed dad even if we wanted to. One answer gaining currency is that fathers should become friends with their children, a buddy-buddy scenario particularly applied to the father-son relationship. It's a seductive notion that's intrinsic to the idea of the cool dad, and a deeply flawed one.

An early wake-up call to any new father is to recognize that, no matter how hip you are – and hipness, as someone remarked, is not a state of mind, it's a fact of life – you're no longer cool. There's a tendency, especially in the early days of parenthood, to fool yourself that you're going to carry on as normal. There's no reason, goes this fantasy, why kids have to interrupt that desirable single lifestyle – other people make too much of it. One result is the spectacle of mothers and fathers showing up to clubs and parties with their papoose strapped on to backs and fronts in some third-world sarong, there to be exposed to the usual mixture of sound-systems, smoke and babble. You soon learn. An effort to catch the latest Hollywood hot-ticket while my partner struggled to breast-feed our three-month-old son in the back row of the local cinema was one experiment we never tried to repeat. Nor does it take long to discover that it is impossible to hang loose and watch the world pass by with the quizzical detachment of the arch-hipster when your two-year-old is on the pavement throwing a wobbler about his sweetie wrapper.

Inevitably, standards of dress take a sharp dive with the advent of fatherhood. No matter how in vogue your new jacket, it isn't going to cut the same dash toting a large patch of regurgitated banana on both shoulders. After a while you find yourself assessing prospective purchases not by their cut but by whether coat pockets can comfortably hold a bottle of lukewarm milk and a packet of chocolate digestives, and shirts stand up to the loving embrace of a pair of tiny, jam-smeared mitts over breakfast. Trousers should ideally come with a special hose-down feature for the removal of muddy stains from the trailing feet of carried kids. Sunglasses, there to be pulled from your face and thrown beneath the wheels of passing motorcycles, should ideally come in non-scratch titanium. Ties – made-to-measure nose-wipes for the porta-tot – must be donned and removed at the front door. So far, the rag trade has been strangely slow to cotton on to the marketing possibilities of designer-dad ranges.

The grim realities of fatherhood – let's put the unabashed joys to one side for the moment – should by now have stemmed the steady wash of magazine articles extolling the cool condition of modern dad-dom. This fantasy, which grew legs around the time of the appearance of the celebrated Athena poster showing a bare-chested male hunk carrying a naked baby, continues to roll off the production line (mostly written by single women, it seems). Along with it comes the canard that women find fatherhood sexy, and that a man with a small child in tow is going to be the magnet for gaggles of adoring females; a sure-fire puller in short. In my experience the opposite holds true. Women, for various reasons, sensibly give men with small children the widest of berths. Single women take one look at this sad, baggy-eyed specimen of manhood and write him off as either already taken or enmeshed in a muddle of divorce and custody proceedings.

Young mothers are even less sympathetic. Their attitude runs from 'He's a man, he doesn't really know how to handle kids' to 'Let him see how hard it is' to 'Very nice, but he's only doing it because it's the mother's day off'. As for fellow fathers – forget it. A collection of mothers at the supermarket or the one o'clock club will quickly start chatting among themselves, comparing notes on their offspring, but the day when blokes bond by baby remains a long way off. Pushing our kids on the swings alongside other dads, we're simply too wrapped up in our own worlds, too embarrassed by our displays of delight and sensitivity, to start talking to each other. Rightly or wrongly, that sort of behaviour is not yet in our genes.

A new generation of non-absent fathers is discovering what women have long maintained: that child care is no piece of cake. It's immensely rewarding at times, of course, but it precludes doing most of the things we'd rather be spending our time on – our work, for example. Like their mothers and grandmothers before them, fathers are increasingly being asked to sideline their careers if they want to spend time with their kids. The demands of the modern workplace, with its unspoken insistence that its salary-slaves prove their allegiance to the company by putting in long hours of overtime, ensure that having a career and being a parent are increasingly incompatible. According to the Institute of Management, the majority of successful men feel that their children are adversely affected by the pattern of their working lives.

Most parents realize, too, that, present or not, they are in some way damaging their children psychologically. The old confidence that mum and dad did indeed know best has evaporated under the revelations of twentieth-century psychology concerning the unconscious power struggles between parents and children. Philip Larkin's celebrated lines – *'They fuck you up, your mum and dad. / They may not mean to, but they do.'* – have become a mantra that haunts the modern parent. The knowledge that we pass on our failings to our children whether we are aware of it or not has left many parents with a deep sense of guilt.

It's hardly surprising if fathers now try to sidestep the uncomfortable psychological transactions that go on within the family. Wouldn't it be nice if we could all just be friends and avoid the whole unpleasant farrago of bitterness and recrimination? For a while, as a father, this seems possible. We bond with our infants, even tolerate their hurtful rejection of us around the 'terrible twos', when the baby in them is supplanted by the brat and they assert their own identity with a litany of 'No' and 'I don't like you'. For several years after that it's possible to enjoy a fruitful and rewarding time with both sons and daughters, providing you can be around enough, and can strike the right balance between parental authority and human vulnerability.

The reckoning of the teenage years can't be avoided, however. The challenge for the current generation of fathers is how to provide the oedipal wall without tipping over into old-fashioned patriarchy. But provide it we must. Opting to be a cool dad, to try to be our children's friend, is a massive abdication of this responsibility. Ultimately, it's just a different way to be an absent father, and possibly as damaging. Robert Bly, in *The Sibling Society*, links the absence of fathering to the growth of 'a society of orphans'. With fathers missing and no experience of the oedipal wall, suggests Bly, 'millions of males linger in a dangerous, frightening and inarticulate fantasy world ... Some sons are so frightened of anger they repress it entirely. Others, with no better modelling, become violent.'

The force of this reckoning came home to me on a couple of occasions recently. One was when I interviewed Blur's Damon Albarn, one of the nineties' biggest pop stars, alongside his father Keith, who as a young man in the late sixties had made something of a name for himself as a whiz-kid architect and designer of what are now called installations (but which back then were referred to as 'environments'). Here was a dazzling example of a 'cool dad' from the sixties, of whom his celebrity son was justifiably proud. Yet, it turned out, Damon's teenage years had been anything but cool.

'It was difficult when we had a young stud in the house' admitted Albarn senior, 'taking the piss quite mercilessly about the sixties, but you had to give space for that, though I can't pretend it was easy. There were some classic confrontations, but we've always hit it off. I'm obviously pleased that Damon has done well, that he's done his own thing and done it effectively, but, without being too sentimental about it, I'm just grateful that now we can get on as two blokes.'

Nearer to home, and therefore more striking, was the reckoning between a friend and his son. I'd watched this boy grow up and remained close to his father throughout. If anyone deserved the title of 'cool dad' it was him, with his immaculate clothes sense, collection of vintage soul records and extensive knowledge of everything from mediaeval church architecture to the marques of Ford saloons. He'd bonded long and well with his son, turned him into as big a fan of the local football club as he was, and stood on the touch line of the school playing field cheering as his boy, a tricky midfielder, scored winning goals. He'd endured the sullen silences and unexpected hostilities of his son's teenage years with an admirable mixture of stoicism and well-directed firmness. His son had turned eighteen, a bright, well-balanced young man; a credit to his parents, whom he loved and respected.

A year or so later this same young man was relating to me the elation of seeing his beloved team win promotion on the last day of the season. 'It was brilliant, we invaded the pitch, me and my mates were all leaping about in the centre circle when I looked round – and it was only my bleedin' dad coming over, wasn't it? What a cringe.'

Knowing the two parties in this episode brought home to me the impossibility of a father being best friends with his children. Even if it doesn't result in any psychological damage, there's something demeaning about the effort. It's inappropriate. It's an invasion of your kids' space. It's a cringe. Being a cool dad is, in the last analysis, profoundly uncool.

I recalled these stories as I tried to explain to my bachelor friend down the pub about the realities of fatherhood. 'It must be great to have a cool dad,' he said.

'Hmmm, how many times do you want to hear the Babylon Zoo album?' I shot back.

'Actually none,' he admitted.

Exactly. Dads, by definition, are not cool.